GENDER AND THE HISTORIAN

GENDER AND THE HISTORIAN

JOHANNA ALBERTI

An imprint of **Pearson Education**

Harlow, England · London · New York · Reading, Massachusetts · San Francisco
Toronto · Don Mills, Ontario · Sydney · Tokyo · Singapore · Hong Kong · Seoul
Taipei · Cape Town · Madrid · Mexico City · Amsterdam · Munich · Paris · Milan

Pearson Education Limited
Head Office:
Edinburgh Gate
Harlow CM20 2JE
Tel: +44 (0)1279 623623
Fax: +44 (0)1279 431059

London Office:
128 Long Acre
London WC2E 9AN
Tel: +44 (0)20 7447 2000
Fax: +44 (0)20 7240 5771
Website: www.history-minds.com

First published in 2002

© Pearson Education 2002

The right of Johanna Alberti to be identified as Author
of this Work has been asserted by her in accordance
with the Copyright, Designs and Patents Act 1988.

ISBN 0 582 40463 0

British Library Cataloguing in Publication Data
A CIP catalogue record for this book can be obtained from the British Library

10 9 8 7 6 5 4 3 2 1

Typeset in 11/13pt Baskerville MT by Graphicraft Limited, Hong Kong
Printed in Malaysia, LSP

The Publishers' policy is to use paper manufactured from sustainable forests.

CONTENTS

ACKNOWLEDGEMENTS

The author would like to acknowledge Clive Emsley as the initiator of this volume. He also read it through in draft and offered encouraging and constructive comments which were immensely valuable. She is delighted to acknowledge extensive assistance from Sam Alberti in checking all things checkable on the world wide web. Irene Dunn at the Robinson Library, University of Newcastle, has been, as always, unfailingly helpful.

CHAPTER ONE

Woman as a force in history

This book examines the writing of historians of women from 1969 to 1999.
The title of the book reflects a change in the angle from which the history
of women has been viewed during this period. Gender, Jane Flax has
declared, 'is a category that feminist theorists have constructed to analyze
certain relations in our cultures and experiences. The concept must therefore reflect our questions, desires, and needs'.[1] The questions, desires and
needs which led to the widespread use of the word gender in studies by
historians of women are varied and complex. Joan Scott suggested that
one motivation was the desire to gain 'academic legitimacy' because the
term 'women's history' contained a threat to the widely accepted view that
women were not 'valid historical subjects', and was associated with the
assumed stridency of feminism.[2] Her own use of the term was fuelled by
a determination to transform the discipline of history. Later chapters will
explore in more detail the emergence of 'gender history' from 'women's
history'.

In this introduction I want to provide some sense of the writing that has
preceded the work of historians of women during the past thirty years. The
context, in which the wave of writing which this book covers took place,
was one in which men dominated writing of history and defined what
historians should and could do. The customs of history writing and the
justification for the historian's craft, which were current when the work
covered by this book began, will be given a necessarily cursory summary.
Alongside this narrative will be placed a selection of the ways early historians
of women have been presented to the modern reader by the current generation of historians of women. There is included within this selection a more
detailed description of the writings of three women historians of women
who wrote in the first half of the twentieth century: Alice Clark, Ivy Pinchbeck

and Mary Beard. My purpose is to place some of the ideas put forward by recent historians of women within a broader context.

The form in which history writing has appeared differs from one period to another. History as we practise it today has its roots in the nineteenth century: historians of the generation who were teaching in the sixties – the early period of the expansion of university education in the Western world – based their practice firmly on nineteenth-century traditions. In particular, the historian Leopold von Ranke has cast a long shadow over the work of historians since the second half of that century. Ranke worked at a time when historians were faced with a 'deluge of information'.[3] His most innovative conception for the practice of history was his insistence that historians should use contemporary documents. Reacting against the writing of history which drew moral lessons about the past, he asserted that the task of the historian was to view the past in a detached manner. If this task was rigorously pursued then he believed that it was possible to narrate the events of the past *'wie es eigentlich gewesen'* (as they actually happened.) The historian, in this perspective, is simply a mirror for the events of the past, albeit one that selects what it reflects. This approach to history is one that has persisted.

Ranke's assertion of the ability of historians to reinscribe the past on to the pages of the present co-existed with another way of seeing the work of a historian which has had less of a powerful influence in the last one hundred years, but has never been totally superseded. However, history as a creation of the historian, a story or a tale, literary history, has deep roots in the earliest known human cultures. In this tradition the quality of the telling is vitally important, although no tale is told without a purpose. Usually histories were used by those with religious or secular power to justify their positions. But groups of people without much power could also use the telling of history for their own purposes. This is a tradition to which the writing of the history of women has strong links. Bonnie Smith has written that 'Without a historian any group remains oppressed, living in "silence", "bonds", and "suffering", until that moment when, as in Whig history, a historical narrative reveals its struggle for liberation.' Smith sees the history of women as 'sharing many traits with Whig history of the past or working-class and black history today, the history of women maintains its affinity, however, weakened, with an epic or romantic tradition'.[4]

Bonnie Smith and other historians of women have been concerned to trace the roots of their practice in an earlier age. Smith's goal in doing this was to 'link women scholars to the historiography of women' by tracing 'a kind of genealogy of women's historiography parallel to that of better-known men'. She has provided a thorough and assertive examination of the contributions of women's historians to history writing. Nathalie Zemon

Davis traced the history of women in history back to Plutarch's 'little bio-graphies of virtuous women', a *genre* of writing on 'women worthies' which she followed up to the nineteenth century.[5] Bonnie Smith agreed that modern historical writing by and about both men and women depended on the biographical mode, but suggested that historians faced problems in writing about great women because their contribution could rarely 'be narrated by the toting up of achievements' and tended to be a considera-tion of their contribution to changing moral standards.[6] Perhaps as a result of these problems, they 'found a more sophisticated alternative in social history', in the exploration of 'the private space in which women could be found'.[7] Lucy Salmon, an American historian working at the beginning of the twentieth century, challenged the exclusion of private sources from his-torical research and used source material found in backyards and kitchens. One study by Salmon examined the fan as a clue to social history.[8] So historians of women who later studied the domestic and the so-called 'trivial' were not breaking entirely new ground. Another social historian, Georgiana Hill, writing *Women in English Life from Medieval to Modern Times* in the late nineteenth century, anticipated a later debate when she wrote that she found no 'unvarying progress from age to age' in the condition of women, despite the progress supposedly characteristic of English political life.[9] Histories which attempted to assess women's status within society were considering women in relation to men: Zemon Davis traces the awareness that 'relations between the sexes should not be perceived as essentially unchanging features of the European past' to late eighteenth-century and nineteenth-century writers, including Engels.[10]

In the nineteenth, as in the second half of the twentieth century, the impetus behind writing women's history was driven by political consid-erations – whether feminist or socialist – but also by historical curiosity. Georgiana Hill was a suffragist: the Victorian women's movement, like its successor in the second half of the twentieth century, provided an impetus for historians of women. On the other side of the Atlantic, the women's movement was stimulating the compilation of women's 'contributions' to history from Margaret Fuller's *Women in the Nineteenth Century* (1844) to Frances Willard and Mary Livermore's *American Women* (1897). Fuller challenged women's alleged inferiority by describing the lives of strong and noble women from classical times onwards. Finding heroines from the past was the starting point for a challenge to the dominant ideology which saw women as of no historical consequence. As Anna Davin has put it, this sort of history can 'serve to provide inspiration, through examples of long injustice, or through evidence which counters stereotypes and assertions of inevitable female destiny, or through golden visions of erstwhile equality or even power'.[11] A more academic drive led to the inclusion of women within general studies of the labouring poor or in collections of community rites and custom. Zemon Davis notes in the late nineteenth and early twentieth century the appearance in Europe of serious studies 'in which the status, activities, and consciousness of women are examined – and not always just of upper-class women – for a manageable period, such as the Middle Ages or the Renaissance'.[12]

The connection of women with moral developments did not disappear. The suffrage movement led to a degree of panic that women might lose their qualities as moral arbiters and protectors of the home. A book entitled *The Women of the Renaissance: A Study of Feminism* by a French historian extolled the intelligence and personal force which lay behind the 'true sweetness, true goodness' of women, but called upon them to 'renounce public life!'. He was prepared to 'Let mannish women, if they must, turn doctors, and womanish women turn priests!'[13] Biographers of prominent women used their narratives of the moral stance of their subjects to criticise male values. Writers who hypothesised the existence of an idealised matriarchy in the ancient world pushed this perspective back into the past. Here lay the antecedents of the golden age debates which would engage women historians in the 1980s. One such writer was Jane Harrison who did not assert the existence of a full-blown matriarchy, but did suggest that evidence pointed to 'the presence in the ancient world of a feminine culture of justice and pacifism interwoven with rivalling warlike institutions'.[14]

Jane Harrison was one of a handful of women scholars in the early twentieth century who held an academic post; in her case in Cambridge. However, it is clear that such a position was not a necessary stepping stone to archival research: June Purvis pointed out that some of the nineteenth-century historians, for example Agnes and Elizabeth Strickland who wrote *Lives of the Queens of England from the Norman Conquest*, based their studies on the original documents.[15] It is too easy to make patronising assumptions about the limitations of an earlier generation of historians. In order to avoid the pitfall of condescension and to clarify the differences between the methods and assumptions of earlier historians, Nathalie Zemon Davis has identified what those historians did and what her own contemporaries would do differently. Alice Clark's *Working Life of Women in the Seventeenth Century* is a book which very many historians of women, and, of course, in particular early modern historians, have used as a benchmark. Zemon Davis described how Clark 'went to the sources' like any historian of the 1970s, including studies of archival material such as judicial, administrative and financial records as well as personal material and prescriptive literature; she 'spelled out the differences among her working women'; she distinguished between legal and other prescriptive images of women and the experience and behaviour of women, and her work was informed by theory: that a 'woman's independence ... was a function of the full realization of her productive powers, biological, educational, and economic'. Finally, she respected her subjects, 'treating them neither as passive victims of historical injustice nor as constant heroines struggling to change society'.[16] Additions to these qualities which Davis argued that a historian of women writing in the 1970s would provide were the use of demography, and in particular the conclusions of studies of the complex and changing nature of families. The use of statistics in general would tighten up Clark's 'impressionistic' use of figures. Davis's contemporaries would be concerned with the erotic and sexual activities of their subjects. These are additional to the work of Clark: the one significant difference that Davis identified was the need to study men and women together, for her version of the goal of the historian of women was 'to understand the significance of the *sexes*, of gender groups in the historical past'.[17]

Any reading of Clark's work would accord with Zemon Davis's recognition that she was not only a precursor of the modern historian of woman but also a practitioner of a craft which is very close to that of her successors; indeed, I would argue, closer than Davis acknowledged. She consciously challenged the invisibility of women in history, and shared later perceptions of the reasons for that invisibility, the regarding of women 'as a static factor in social developments'.[18] She placed her study consciously in what we would call an interdisciplinary location adjacent to sociology and psychology, and she challenged male categorisations of women's working life, and of 'organisation for production'.[19] Although she is generally associated with the argument that it was economic forces which changed women's lives, she stated in her conclusion: 'If we would understand the effect of the introduction of Capitalism on the social organism, we must remember that the subjection of women to their husbands was the foundation stone of the structure of the community in which Capitalism first made its appearance.'[20] She then described a system of male domination to which later historians would give the name 'patriarchy'. Clark's analysis led her to conclude that the introduction of capitalism took place within this structure and also changed it, and that the changes affected the consciousness of both men and women. On the final pages of the book she identified the emergence of both the private sphere, and 'the organisation of a State which regards the purposes of life solely from the male standpoint'.[21]

I have been struck by a strong sense that many of the ideas which gender historians have put forward in the past thirty years have been expressed by historians in the past: as Bonnie Smith put it, the themes of historians of women from the mid-eighteenth century were 'recapitulated when the history of women received a new impetus in the late 1960s'.[22] The factor which is peculiar to the period, which this book will cover, is the way women's history has become the task of many historians rather than a very select few. The explanation for this lies partly in the fact that many more women were more highly educated than in Clark's time, but also, as Chapter Two will demonstrate, in the emergence of a strong women's movement, itself of course part of the process of social change which led to women's arrival in significant numbers in higher education. The existence of a community of like-minded scholars is also a relevant factor in the development of a new departure in the study of history. It seems unlikely that Alice Clark herself could have done her work without the support of her contemporaries. In order to complete her research Clark was awarded a fellowship at the London School of Economics in 1912. The fellowship had been established by Charlotte Payne Townsend Shaw, the wife of George Bernard Shaw, and was specifically intended for a woman. The previous holder was Eileen Power, and Clark used Power's material on medieval women when assessing her own period. She was supervised by Dr. Lillian Knowles, another medievalist. Two other students from the LSE published works on women's history at around this time: B.L. Hutchin's *Women in Modern Industry* appeared in 1915, and Ivy Pinchbeck's *Women Workers and the Industrial Revolution* in 1930. In her introduction to a book on women in the eighteenth century published in 1989, Bridget Hill wrote:

> When I started this book I was aware that women's history in the eighteenth and early nineteenth century owed much to Ivy Pinchbeck. But as I proceeded the greater became my consciousness of the size of that debt. It is against her work that must be measured the contributions of the last half century to our knowledge and understanding of eighteenth-century working women. My debt to her is immense.[23]

Pinchbeck's conclusions offered a direct challenge to the idea that women's position in history was immutable. 'Economically, women were vitally affected by the industrial revolution.'[24] She provided a lucid perspective on the complex effects of industrialisation on women's lives. For the single working woman, 'the most striking effect of the industrial revolution was her distinct gain in social and economic independence'.[25] Women were better off under the factory system than in domestic service, she concluded, quoting an article by Caroline Foley written in 1894 to the effect that the factory brought out the 'self-respect, self-reliance and courage' of the girls who worked there. The majority of married women, on the other hand, 'lost their economic independence', yet 'it cannot be denied that it immensely improved her domestic conditions'.[26] Pinchbeck was writing at a time when domesticity – a 'home of one's own' – was experienced by working-class women as liberating as much if not more than it was constraining. She was able to write without irony that the path towards the 'assumption that men's wages should be paid on a family basis' marked 'a real advance', and that 'the modern conception' was that 'in the rearing of children and in home-making, the married woman makes an adequate economic contribution'.[27] Pinchbeck illustrated the consequences of industrialisation for middle-class women by comparing 'the vigorous life of the eighteenth-century business woman, travelling about the country in her own interests, with the sheltered existence of the Victorian woman.' But, she added, it was from awareness of their own position, and of the 'economic emancipation of working women', that individuals among the middle-classes were stimulated to demand higher education and training, and the re-admission of women into industry and the professions.[28]

In parallel with these developments in Britain, two notable works by American women historians appeared at this time: *Women in Industry* (1918) by Edith Abbot, and *Colonial Women of Affairs: Women in Business and Professions in America Before 1776* (1931) by Elizabeth Dexter. But the American historian whose work has both inspired and troubled feminist historians in the early years of the recent wave of women's history is Mary Beard whose *Woman as a Force in History* was published in 1946.[29] What has chiefly been remembered from *Woman as a Force in History* is Beard's insistence that all women made an active contribution to history. Beard began in the present, identifying three views of women current at the time: the communist, asserting equality; the fascist, emphasising domesticity, and the democratic, valuing choice. She then looked at women's attitudes towards their sex in the claims for a place for women by three assertive women in the period 1900–46: Charlotte Perkins Gilman (novelist and writer on women in the economy), Carey Thomas (President of Bryn Mawr College) and Eleanor Roosevelt (the wife of the President of the US). Examining a range of men's current views on women she detected no agreement. But she found that writings on the law and on women's history were haunted by the idea of women in subjection. Casting a long look at the history of women from medieval times she echoed those who had seen women as more highly moral than men when she found that 'women were . . . in the main on the side of civilization in the struggle with barbarism'. But she also emphasised the indissoluble links between men and women, for 'civilization . . . occurs in society, and all the agencies used in the process – language, ideas, knowledge, institutions, property, arts and the inventions – are social products, the work of men and women . . .'. For Beard, there was no 'woman question alone, as social philosophers – women and men – have understood from the dawn of reflective thought. It is a human problem'.[30] This was a statement which her contemporaries would have found quite unexceptional: but human all too often meant male. In a review of *Women as a Force in*

History J.H. Hexter asserted that women were not to be found in the places in history which were worthy of study; 'through no conspiracy of the historians, the College of Cardinals, the Consistory of Geneva, the Parliament of England, and the expeditions of Columbus, Vasco da Gama and Drake have been pretty much stag affairs'.[31]

Two earlier books of Beard's – *On Understanding Women* and *America Through Women's Eyes* – were those which, in Bonnie Smith's view, achieved a historical breakthrough: in these two volumes she 'showed quite self-consciously how differently history looked when seen through women's eyes'.[32] Smith's examination of Beard's writing drew out the irony and humour: she 'smiles at the feebleness of men who depended on women's innovations in agriculture, textile construction, and the like to lift "her low-browed male companion above the wild beasts that he hunted with stone and club and devoured in the raw"'.[33] According to Smith, Beard's originality lay not in her search for women in history, but in her use of women's voices and, related to this, her assumption that history was a narrative of 'multiple points of view'. She thus encouraged a shift in the debate about history from facts to interpretation, and retained a faith in the need to write a history which acknowledged diversity but aimed to be universal. Her criticism of the old masters of history such as von Ranke was that they were 'fragmenters'. The tendency for modern historians of women to feel that their project was entirely unprecedented is suggested by Berenice Carroll's comment on Beard's identification of the problem of 'taking man as a measure' as 'curiously close to the rhetoric of women's liberationists today'.[34] Smith, on the other hand, pointed to Beard's refusal to write 'a "feminist" history that focused on "struggle" from a position of invisibility, for that would be . . . writing a feminine version of Whig history'.[35] Bonnie Smith, writing almost a decade after Carroll, and when women's history and indeed the category 'women' was under intense scrutiny, rejected the tendency to create a 'monumental Mary Beard'. To do so, Smith argued, was 'to contradict the spirit of her writing': Mary Beard's presence in historiography is as elusive as women's presence in history.[36]

Most historians writing in the middle of the twentieth century chose their material and worked within a framework whose dimensions were widely accepted both within the academic world and in circles where history was a more populist practice. The task of the historian was still firmly placed within the tradition established by Ranke. Henrietta Leyser recalled (in the introduction to a book on medieval women published in 1995), her 'fascinated horror' as an undergraduate that 'history as an academic discipline was a nineteenth-century invention'.[37] As E.H. Carr described the task proposed by Ranke: 'History consists of a corpus of ascertained facts. The facts are available to the historian in documents, inscriptions and so on, like fish on the fishmonger's slab. The historian collects them, takes them home and cooks and serves them in whatever style appeals to him.'[38] By the mid-twentieth century aspects of this recipe were no longer acceptable to some historians: as E.H. Carr put it: 'Now this clearly will not do.'[39] To illustrate the changing standpoint, he quoted the introduction to the *New Cambridge Modern History*, published in 1957, and written by Professor Sir George Clark. Historians, Clark asserted, 'consider that knowledge of the past has come down through one or more human minds, has been "processed" by them, and therefore cannot consist of elemental and impersonal atoms which nothing can alter . . . The exploration seems to be endless . . .'.[40] Carr's rejection of an absolute objectivity, his awareness of the presence of subjectivity in both historical sources and in the historian, together with his retention of a faith in the significance of history find their echoes in the early work of women historians who are the subject of this book. He stressed the importance of studying the historian before you begin to study the facts. He deemed history to be 'a constantly moving process, with the historian moving within it'.[41] On the other hand, he also rejected relativism, the view that 'because interpretation plays a necessary part in establishing the facts of history, and because no existing interpretation is wholly objective, one interpretation is as good as another', backing this understanding with the image of the mountain which appears different from different angles, but still has one essential shape.[42] And he wanted to rescue history from becoming 'the telling of stories without purpose or significance'.[43] To this end, he retained ideas about cause and effect, but stressed that the historian 'deals in a multiplicity of causes', although he is professionally compelled to prioritise them.[44] He also reconstructed objectivity in a different form from that understood by Ranke, because he thought that a standard of significance was needed by which interpretations could be judged. For Carr, 'objectivity in history does not and cannot rest on some fixed and immovable standard of judgement existing here and now, but only on a standard which is laid up in the future and is evolved as the course of history advances'.[45] He believed then that history could only be written 'by those who find and accept a sense of direction in history itself'.[46]

The idea that a historian should be judged by a standard deeply rooted in the idea of progress would be implicit in the writing of some historians of women. The new wave of historians of women which emerged in the 1960s was linked to a women's movement committed to changing the world for the better. As students, these historians found themselves in an environment which was both sceptical and optimistic, and studying a syllabus which was archaic. Sheila Rowbotham joined Henrietta Leyser at Oxford, in 1961. 'It was very bewildering. We had to read Gibbon, Macaulay, de Tocqueville and Bede the first term, after which we launched into the Romans and

Anglo-Saxons and European diplomatic intrigue in the nineteenth century. The syllabus changes slowly in Oxford, and I suppose we were still being prepared to serve in the early twentieth-century Indian Civil Service or Foreign Office'.[47] It was difficult to study a history which was not about governmental structures and foreign policy, and the points of view of the historians she read were 'never presented as methods of looking at history explicitly, but as objective, unbiased common sense'. It was hard, she found, to question either the content or the method, and questioning the status quo required a confidence which women students, who were a 'tiny minority' were unlikely to find in 'male stronghold' where they were 'subtly taught our place by being told how privileged we were to be there at all'.[48] Before Rowbotham arrived in Oxford, Keith Thomas had run a series of lectures on seventeenth-century women.[49] Thomas remembered later that his colleagues had found the subject bizarre, and that students simply did not turn up to listen.

Generally speaking, women did not appear on the pages of history books in the sixties. A survey of twenty-seven college-level American history text books (published, with two exceptions, in the years 1965 to 1971) found that the number of pages devoted to women rarely topped 1 per cent.[50] Another of the essays in *Liberating Women's History* reviewed books and articles by male American historians about women, mostly within radical movements, including feminism, written between 1963 and 1971. This study found that some of the authors were 'candid about their attitudes towards women, boldly stating that they believe biological differences will always make women unequal'. Others denied such biological determinism but wrote 'in a way which suggests that even if differences do not arise out of biology, they remain immutable'. All the historians, the authors of the study contended, saw women as 'the source of their own oppression'. Even those historians who were critical of American institutions failed to see that there was any change needed as far as women were concerned, and suggested that those women who put their own problems first were allowing their emotions to cloud their judgment. The point of view of these authors was presented not as male, but as objective.[51]

The facts of women's lives were not judged by many historians in the 1950s to be significant. There were isolated, partial challenges to this view. Doris Mary Stenton's *The English Woman in History* (1957) chronicled famous and exceptional women. Stenton's book is very much in the tradition of claiming that exceptional women had lived and made an impact on history. A more than individual exception was the story of women's struggle for the vote which was an aspect of women's history which did receive attention from historians. Suffragists on both sides of the Atlantic wrote their own history, and they were accompanied and followed by books which were informed by 'a certain masculine condescension' according to Roger Fulford whose *Votes for Women (1958)* was intended as a serious study, one which would counteract the tendency of 'the great masters of history . . . to view the efforts of feminists with too much indifference and amusement'.[52] In the following year, Eleanor Flexner's *Century of Struggle: The Woman's Rights Movement in the United States* was published.[53] Its aim – to trace the nineteenth century women's movement from 'scattered beginnings' down to the enactment of the suffrage amendment in 1920 – was, as she admitted in her preface to the revised edition published in 1975, 'not so much ambitious as presumptuous'. Flexner told the story of the individual women and their organisations; a heroic struggle with obstacles and villains to overcome, with triumph the result of the determination and vigour of the women and the support of 'far-seeing and loyal men'.[54] The impact of the British women's suffrage movement on the politics of the period 1866 to 1914 was given serious study by Constance Rover.[55]

In the late sixties two path-breaking articles were published in American journals. In 1966 Barbara Welter examined *The Cult of True Womanhood, 1820–1860* as articulated in sermons and periodicals. Welter related role prescription to social change in mid-nineteenth-century America, defining role socialization as central to both women's history and social history.[56] Welter's article was followed in 1969 by a more critical scrutiny of 'The lady and the mill girl: changes in the status of women in the age of Jackson (1800–1840)' by Gerda Lerner who was to become highly influential in the articulation of the task of the historian of women over the next twenty-five years.[57] The period she studied, was, she maintained, 'one in which decisive changes occurred in the status of American women'. When 'the Revolution had substituted an egalitarian ideology for the hierarchical concepts of colonial life', the 'actual situation' for women had in fact deteriorated. Work outside the home was disapproved of, business and professional opportunities were closed, and their legal status declined relative to that of men. Lerner's argument reads like an American version of Clark and Pinchbeck with the force for change political instead of economic. Lerner continued her study by shifting her focus on to working-class women, and for millgirls in New England, she detected the 'relatively high wages' and 'a relatively high status' which Pinchbeck had identified in England. Lerner was interested in the polarisation of attitudes towards women: the image of 'the lady' as the 'accepted ideal of femininity towards which all women would strive', simply ignored lower class women. The one thing the lady and the mill girl had in common was their disenfranchisement. Where Pinchbeck had looked forward to the liberation of women through education and entry into business and the professions, Lerner detected a sense of political frustration which 'was one of the main factors in the rise of the women's rights movement'. Where Pinchbeck saw middle-class women learning what was possible from the economic independence of the working woman, Lerner saw the concerns of middle-class women dominating the women's rights movement; not until there was cooperation between the mill girl and the lady would they unite to gain female suffrage.

Gerda Lerner identified the influence of middle-class concerns behind what she termed the 'feminist' framework which historians had adopted for the study of women, a framework which led to generalisations about American women which only applied to a particular class of women. As this accusation suggests, Lerner's first writings on women were not inspired specifically by the dawning of a new wave of the women's movement. However, her consciousness that women had been largely ignored was part of the growing realisation by contemporary women of the continued weight of a male-dominated culture on women's freedom of thought. As the 'women's liberation' movement began to stir, so indignation and a growing sense of solidarity between women provided fertile soil for new growth. Carroll Smith-Rosenberg, an American historian who has contributed richly to the writings on approaches to women's history, described her own shift in focus thus: 'My original concern was not with women, but with the ways in which nineteenth-century Americans responded to urbanization and poverty. Only gradually did I recognize that a number of early urban philanthropic institutions were separatist female organizations. Attempting to account for this phenomenon, I was drawn into an analysis of the world view of these female reformers.'[58] She had found that the 'New Women's History' with its emphasis on role discontent and its search for models to explain the relations between role conflict and social change, had led her towards a quite different approach to the subjects of her work. Smith-Rosenberg sees her own re-orientation as 'reinforced' not only by the contemporary women's movement but also by the methodological innovations of the New Social History. The development of demographical techniques such as aggregate data analysis in the 1950s and 1960s made possible detailed family studies which provided a way of studying, as Smith Rosenberg put it, 'the domestic world of the inarticulate, the working class, the immigrant and the black – and even of the women within these groups'. Moreover, social historians began to borrow models and analytic tools from the behavioural sciences to study social structures and social processes such as child-rearing and sexual behaviour in which women were central. Yet all but a few New Social Historians ignored women. The claim that the experience of the powerless and the inarticulate was significant did not necessarily include women within its scope: they were often marginalised because the working class was defined implicitly as male. Even when historians turned to look at the family, it was treated very much as a unit and relations within it remained unexamined. In France, the developments which led to the emergence of the *Annales* school of historians ran in parallel with the emergence of the New Social History in the United States. Named from their journal, *Annales d'Histoire Economique et Sociale*, historians of this persuasion encouraged the writing of histories which were concerned with ordinary life, and also sought to break down the lines of demarcation between historians. Considerable change in the study of history was taking place in the sixties. Into a context where innovation was possible there entered the political force of the women's movement: Chapter Two will look at the impact of this movement on the writing of the history of women.

* * * * * *

The material of this book is arranged chronologically. I want both to give a sense of the growth of the discipline of women's history between the early seventies and the late nineties, and also to point to the way the main themes and ideas have often been present in the writings of historians of women from the beginning of this period, and have persisted, albeit in slightly altered form, until the end. The shape of the development of these ideas is thus a spiral, although this has been difficult to delineate on the page. In Chapter Two the exhilaration, and also the restraints, of the early seventies are described. The two voices which emerge most clearly are those of Gerda Lerner in the USA and Sheila Rowbotham in the UK. Lerner was especially determined that there should be an appropriate conceptual framework for the work of historians of women. She identified early on some of the themes which were to provide a focus for the next thirty years, such as the differences between women and the complex issue of the exercise of power, the agency of women. A rejection of generalisations about women's experience in the past was voiced by the many other historians who wrote the essays and articles which make up the bulk of the writings on women's history in the early seventies. Historians were inspired by the experience of sisterhood in the contemporary women's movement, but this did not mislead them into seeing women as homogenous. Class – especially for British historians – and race were recognised as powerful axes cutting across women's experience of oppression in the past.

From the start, historians of women expected that their work would not just add to the material of history but change it. Chapter Three traces the determination of women on both sides of the Atlantic to place their work firmly in the public arena, and to begin to map out the ways in which the study of women was altering the landscape of history. The significance of the relationship between men and women in the past, and the way their histories interlocked, were identified as essential aspects of any theoretical framework appropriate to the history of women. The issue of how power was exercised both over women and by them was debated. Men's power over women, generalised as patriarchy, was subject to differing interpretations. There was criticism of the idea that patriarchy was based on biological differences between men and women and was therefore not subject to change. From the USA Joan Kelly offered a 'double vision' for feminist historians, one which would link the study of patriarchal forms of production with the domination of women through sexual and psychological forms of power. Both forms of power were observed in operation in the formation of a 'woman's culture' in nineteenth-century America. Whether feminism grew from such a culture was the subject of fascination and some disagreement. The convergence of historians of women from either side of the Atlantic was cogently described by Jane Lewis in a summary of the development and current shape of the discipline published in 1981. Lewis was then a lecturer in social administration; her presence in the field of history demonstrating the way women's history was to appeal to academics across the disciplines. One discipline which was to have an impact on the work of some historians of women from the late seventies on was psychoanalysis, and in particular the work of Jacques Lacan.

Jane Lewis made productive use of the concept of gender in her article: the fruitfulness of this broad and flexible notion was fast becoming apparent. By the early eighties the American historian Joan Scott was dissatisfied with what she saw as only the faint impression made by historians of women on the wider discipline. She became convinced that the way to go beyond adding women to the content of history and in addition to alter its shape was to make use of the concept of gender as a category of analysis. This conviction provides the framework for Chapter Four. Scott understood the term both as constituting relations between women and men, and as a way of signifying relationships of power. The historian's task was to trace the process of the work of gender as it operated and changed over time. Scott's emphasis on gender led her to an understanding of her discipline which was primarily concerned with ideas and language. The links between the methodology of the historian and the literary critic were affirmed by other American historians, including Carroll Smith Rosenberg. Meanwhile other practitioners from a widening geographical area were continuing the work of rescuing women in the past from obscurity.

Confidence in the validity of the enterprise of women's history was more apparent than faith in its ability to survive within the broader discipline. In the late eighties, Michelle Perrot still saw the practice of history in France as a male preserve, and the position of her own subject as fragile and reversible. She was dubious about any claims that historians of women were changing the perspective of their fellow practitioners. Despite Perrot's doubts, there were indisputable signs of growth in the status and volume of work on women in the late eighties. There was also broad agreement on what that work constituted: the recognition that women did indeed have a history of their own; the demonstration that gender was a powerful determining force, and the argument that these perspectives would make a difference to historical interpretations. That there was a political agenda behind the writing of women's history was acknowledged by many practitioners, and asserted critically by some well-known male historians. Their criticisms expressed concern about the threat to scholarly rigour posed by those who adopted a feminist perspective. Linda Gordon, an American historian whose work focused on women's control of their bodies, pointed out that feminists were not alone in using history to sustain political vision, and argued that the relationship between academic rigour and the political aspirations of feminism created of necessity a fruitful tension. An exemplary demonstration of this creative tension was Leonore Davidoff and Catherine Hall's *Family Fortunes*, a work which was based on rigorous research and informed by a feminist understanding.

Feminism was itself subject to a variety of different interpretations in the late eighties, as the women's movement became at the same time both more successful in achieving its aims and less distinct in its identity. Contemporary experience may have informed the work of those historians of women who were examining the political history of the women's movement of the late nineteenth and early twentieth century. Some of this historical work is described in Chapter Four: Chapter Five picks up the theme of increasing diversity in the discipline of women's history. Another theme of Chapter Five is the impact of the ideas of Foucault and Derrida, in particular the tool of deconstruction. This is a term which is often used loosely to mean unpicking the meaning of a text, but in the work of Derrida has the more precise definition of analysing the way differences – specifically binary oppositions where there is no overlapping of meaning – are made use of for particular purposes. Some historians of women found such devices – loosely labelled 'postmodernist' – liberating. One such was Mary Poovey whose versatile and enthusiastic embracing of deconstruction as a tool led her to use terms new to historians, such as 'symbolic economy', 'fabric' (in place of narrative) and 'cultural scripts'. Despite her perception that the idea of the individual was problematic, Poovey did not abandon a perspective on history which saw the women she was studying as real. There were, as other literary critics also acknowledged, differences in intention between the writing of historical and literary narratives, so that the tools of the literary critic might be destructive of the enterprise of history. In particular the idea that a historian could and should attempt to explain the past seemed to be under threat.

From today's perspective it would seem that historians of women were in the forefront of theoretical innovations in the discipline. Yet Joan Scott continued to express her dissatisfaction with the lack of impact of feminists on her discipline. One factor which may explain this paradox was the continued focus on the study of 'women's culture'. Instead of emphasising women's absence from public life, historians should, it was argued by a group of French historians, re-evaluate the political events in which women participated. An early exclusion of women from a rather differently constituted public sphere emerged from studies of medieval and early modern women which examined the nature of women's subordination to men within and outside the family: the extent and nature of these changes in the pattern of gender relationships was debated. A commitment to the feminist impulse behind women's history was still apparent in the late eighties, especially in the writings of Judith Bennett on medieval women. Gisela Bock, whose work focuses on the twentieth century, warned of the dangers of projecting a modern conception of what constituted positive change for women in the past. Bock also saw a threat in the increasingly fashionable use of the concept gender which was in danger, she argued, of becoming itself a gender-neutral discourse. She welcomed the study of gender where it consisted in an examination of previously neglected relationships. Bennett was also wary of 'gender as meaning' when it led to a neglect of the material in history.

The early nineties was a period when the implications of the challenge to ideas about the validity of writing about the individuality and agency of the historical subject was widely and thoughtfully considered. Chapter Six describes the determination of historians of women to accept the intellectual rewards which deconstruction offered – its subversion of lazily accepted categories, for example – without losing the ability to interpret, and to make choices. Gisela Bock's warning voice was heard again, and welcomed by some historians who found her ideas less hegemonic than Joan Scott's. Concern was expressed about the implications for women's history of the development of a hierarchy within the discipline as it grew and some at least of its practitioners became part of the academic establishment. The sense among British historians of women was that they still remained largely on the margins – potentially still a fruitful place to be. Those who had indubitably been excluded even from that marginal space were making insistent claims to be heard: historians of black women. The relationship between race and gender was the focus of a burst of writing, and there was belated acknowledgement of the imperialist nature of nineteenth-century feminism. These developments occurred, unsurprisingly, at a time when the multicultural nature of British society was also being recognised.

The controversy over the validity and usefulness of the concept 'patriarchy' continued, with an increasing emphasis on its historical variability.

The extent and the chronology of changes in women's lives was also the focus of a challenge: when were women forced into the private sphere, and how effective was this patriarchal strategy? The categories of public and private were subject to scrupulous analysis. It is relevant that the nineties was a time when women were present in larger numbers in contemporary 'public' life; that is to say in the media, and in the business, political and academic worlds. It was also a time when younger women were challenging the goals of feminism as defined by an older generation. This challenge took place in parallel with the expression of fears that a cultural misogynist backlash was in evidence. Some historians found it difficult to detect much damage to the male bastions of their discipline. There was a sense in which the historian of women was still working within the cultural domination which they were exposing in the past. The partial replacement of 'women's history' by 'gender history' was in itself arguably a sign of the continued marginality of women.

Chapter Seven begins with a review of historians' writings on masculinity, in particular the work of John Tosh whose research has focused on the relationship between men and the private sphere in the nineteenth century. Other writers on masculinity were confirming the view that the category 'men' was as unstable as 'women'. There was as yet no 'meta-narrative' in which detailed studies of masculinity could be placed: the need for such narratives in the history of women was also asserted. Once such historian, Olwen Hufton, in a book covering three hundred years, asserted the need to emphasise the material forces which shaped women's lives. Hufton did not deny the value of more detailed studies which were more tied to textual analysis. The 'linguistic turn' was the phrase now widely used to encapsulate the approach which emphasised language and representation and cast doubt on the ability of historian to narrate events of the past as they actually happened. An angry attack on the 'linguistic turn' which asserted that it was devised by men and adopted by women who wanted to advance their careers appeared in 1994. The author of the attack, Joan Hoff, argued that the effects of the adoption of this approach was to impose the brittleness of the present onto the past, and to blunt the political edge of the writing of women's history.

While there was resistance from others besides Hoff to the ideas and practices which she rejected, the early nineties was perhaps a watershed of anxiety concerning the threat posed by the 'linguistic turn'. By the mid-nineties there was plenty of evidence that historians of women were making use of the analytical methods and insights developed by feminists, linguists, philosophers and anthropologists without losing touch with the material and without abandoning the political project of women's history. There was widespread acceptance that historians relied inescapably on ideas contained in the concepts experience, agency and individual, however unstable they might prove to be. Lyndal Roper, an Australian-born historian of the early modern period, moved from a position in which she understood gender as a product only of cultural and linguistic practice to an exploration of the psychic and bodily reality of sexual difference. She pointed out that the preoccupation of feminist historians tended to be those of the particular moment and saw the mid-nineties as a time when some illusions about what could be 'made anew' were being cast aside.

At the end of Chapter Seven there is a review of recent work by some of the most stimulating and productive historians of women of the past thirty years: Gerda Lerner, Leonore Davidoff, Joan Scott and Penny Summerfield. They bear witness to the enormous impact that historians of women have had on the discipline, particularly during the period covered by this book. Women's history has altered the way history has been perceived, initiating theoretical and philosophical debates in a way almost (the exception is the influx of Marxism) unprecedented in Anglo-Saxon historiography. Alongside this methodological innovation and brilliance has run a steady thread of writing based on scrupulous research and well-judged interpretation. This book attempts to do justice to at least some of the practitioners of the recent wave of conceptualising and writing the history of gender.

Notes and references

1. Jane Flax, 'The end of innocence', in Judith Butler and Joan Scott, eds., *Feminists Theorize the Political* (London, 1992), p. 434.

2. Joan Wallach Scott, *Gender and the Politics of History* (New York, 1988), p. 31.

3. J.H. Plumb, *The Death of the Past* (Basingstoke, Hants, 1969), p. 131.

4. Bonnie G. Smith, 'The contribution of women to modern historiography in Great Britain, France, and the United States, 1750–1940', *American Historical Review*, 89 (1986), pp. 709–32.

5. Natalie Zemon Davis, '"Women's History" in transition: the European case', *Feminist Studies*, 3:3/4 (Spring/Summer, 1976), p. 83.

6. Smith (1986), pp. 714–16.

7. Ibid., p. 718.

8. Ibid., pp. 725–6.

9. Ibid., p. 719.

10. Zemon Davis (1976), p. 85.

11. Anna Davin, 'Redressing the balance or transforming the art? The British Experience', in S. Jay Kleinberg (ed.), *Retrieving Women's History: Changing Perceptions of the Role of Women in Politics and Society* (Oxford and New York, 1988), pp. 61–2.

12. Zemon Davis (1976), p. 83.

13. R. de Maulde la Claviere, *The Women of the Renaissance: A Study of Feminism* (London, 1900), p. 502.

14. Smith (1986), pp. 722–3.

15. June Purvis (ed.), *Women's History: Britain 1850–1945: an introduction* (London, 1995), p. 3.

16. Zemon Davis (1976), pp. 82–3.

17. Ibid., p. 88.

18. Alice Clark, *The Working Life of Women in the Seventeenth Century* (London, 1919), p. 1.

19. Ibid., p. 6.

20. Ibid., p. 306.

21. Ibid., p. 308.

22. Smith (1986), p. 726.

23. Bridget Hill, *Women, Work and Sexual Politics in Eighteenth Century England* (London and New York, 1989), p. vii.

24. Ivy Pinchbeck, *Women Workers and the Industrial Revolution* (London, 1930), p. 312.

25. Ibid., p. 313.

26. Ibid., pp. 307–8.

27. Ibid., pp. 312–13.

28. Ibid., p. 316.

29. Mary Beard, *Woman as a Force in History: A Study in Tradition and Realities* (New York, 1946).

30. Ibid., p. 331.

31. *New York Times* (17 March 1946), p. 5.

32. Smith (1986), p. 726.

33. Bonnie Smith, 'Seeing Mary Beard', *Feminist Studies*, 10 (1984), pp. 399–418.

34. Berenice A. Carroll, 'Mary Beard's *Woman as a Force in History*: A Critique', in Berenice A. Carroll, ed., *Liberating Women's History* (Urbana and Chicago, Illinois, London, 1976), p. 33.

35. Smith (1984), p. 407.

36. Ibid., p. 414.

37. Henrietta Leyser, *Medieval Women: A Social History of Women in England 450–1500* (London, 1995), p. ix.

38. E.H. Carr, *What Is History?* (London, 1961), p. 3.

39. Ibid., p. 4.

40. Ibid., p. 2.

41. Ibid., p. 128.

42. Ibid., p. 21.

43. Ibid., p. 119.

44. Ibid., pp. 83–4.

45. Ibid., p. 124.

46. Ibid., p. 126.

47. Sheila Rowbotham, *Dreams and Dilemmas* (London, 1983), p. 168.

48. Ibid., p. 170.

49. Keith Thomas, *Observer* (8 August 1993).

50. Dolores Barracano Schmidt and Earl Robert Schmidt, 'The invisible woman: the historian as professional magician', in Carroll, ed. (1976), pp. 42–55.

51. Linda Gordon, Persis Hunt, Elizabeth Pleck, Rochelle Goldberg Ruthchild, and Marcia Scott, 'Historical phallacies: sexism in American historical writing', in ibid., pp. 70–1.

52. Roger Fulford, *Votes for Women: The Story of a Struggle* (London, 1958), pp. 10–11.

53. Eleanor Flexner, *Century of Struggle: The Woman's Rights Movement in the United States* (Cambridge, Mass., London, 1959).

54. Ibid., p. xi.

55. Constance Rover, *Women's Suffrage and Party Politics in Britain 1866–1914* (London, Toronto, 1967).

56. Barbara Welter, 'The cult of true womanhood: 1800–1860', *American Quarterly*, 18 (Summer, 1966), pp. 151–74.

57. Gerda Lerner, 'The lady and the mill girl: changes in the status of women in the age of Jackson', *Midcontinent American Studies Journal*, 10 (Spring 1969), pp. 5–15.

58. Carroll Smith-Rosenberg, 'The new woman and the new history', *Feminist Studies*, 3 (Autumn, 1975a), pp. 185–98.

CHAPTER TWO

A moment in history 1969–75

'The striking fact about the historiography of women is the general neglect of the subject by historians.' Gerda Lerner's statement was made in an article published in 1969 and entitled *New Approaches to the Study of Women in American History.*[1] Lerner was a Jewish refugee from Nazi Germany who had trained as a historian in her forties: her experience of being an outsider was to inform her awareness of women's position in history. Her explanation for the 'general neglect' of women in history was that they were 'outside the power structure', or at best 'their relationship to power was implicit and peripheral and could easily be passed over as insignificant'. She acknowledged that women had received some attention in the 1960s from social historians, but pointed out that what interest there was focused on 'their position in the family and on their social status'. By 1969 she was a member of the faculty of Sarah Lawrence College, and had in that same year published 'The lady and the mill girl', the germinal article referred to in Chapter 1. Her consciousness of the absence of women from writings on history, and from academia and her preparedness to express this awareness made her one of the first voices to be heard in what was to become a fast growing and dynamic discipline.

The early seventies was a period of intense excitement for historians of women. The growing awareness of the significance and extent of the field which lay before them was exhilarating. The format of publications in this period tended to be articles and essays: collections of essays dominate the landscape, although several introductory books began to break the ground. Themes and issues which would be debated over the ensuing years rapidly appeared: the impact of industrialisation on women's lives; questions of oppression and agency; the relationship between feminism and women's history. Historians of women openly expressed their concern with current preoccupations in their work. They noted the need to find a new and more appropriate periodisation for women's history; they emphasised the diversity of women's experience and the dangers of generalising and they began to grapple with the elusiveness of the concept of power. Some historians of women, especially those working in Britain, adopted a Marxist framework, but they and others were not content to remain within a structure which did not seem to fit the material which they were unearthing.

In *New Approaches to the Study of Women in American History*, Lerner looked briefly at nineteenth-century writings on the history of women which she understood as informed by 'the feminist viewpoint', and placed them in categories: one such was the search for and celebration of women's contribution, and another narratives of the women's movement. She identified a moralistic bias in such writings which resulted in the exclusion of those feminists seen as too radical, and an understanding of the history of women exclusively as a struggle against oppression. She demanded a 'new conceptual framework for dealing with the subject of women in American history' because the 'feminist frame of reference has become archaic and fairly useless'. To us this may seem a startling comment, given the widely accepted association of women's history with feminism. Lerner clearly still saw the feminist perspective as a limited one, although she recognised the emergence of a 'new feminism'. She wanted the history of women to be examined from 'a historical perspective and understanding', and by implication did not expect feminism to provide such a perspective. Lerner emphasised the complexity of the subject, which she saw as 'full of paradoxes which elude precise definitions and defy synthesis'. She thought that it was difficult to 'conceptualise women as a group, since they are dispersed throughout the population'; women were 'at various times and places a majority of the population, yet their status was that of an oppressed minority'. They were excluded from power, yet within families they were 'closer to actual power than many a man'. Women were among the exploited and the exploiters; they were conservative within their communities, yet 'their organisations were frequently allied with the most radical and even revolutionary causes and entered alliances with the very groups threatening the status quo'. Women's paradoxical behaviour was matched by the contradictions of their status. They were honoured as mothers, essential to the survival of the group, and yet they were deprived of an income of their own. Lerner's suggestions for a fresh approach started from the premise that '"Women" is too vast and diffuse to serve as a valid point of departure.' The only valid 'statement about women in general' in her view concerned their political status. She advocated the study of the woman's rights movement as 'part of the total story', and, rejecting the '"oppressed group model"', challenged the idea that women in the past were powerless: 'My research has

led me to believe that they wielded considerable power and in the middle
of the nineteenth century even political power.' She drew attention to the
distinction between the ideas of society about women's proper place, and
'what was actually woman's status at that time'. Finally, she considered how
judgments could be made about 'the contribution of women', and called for
the devising of a different scale of measurement from that employed by men.

The breadth of scope of this essay by Gerda Lerner indicates her acute
awareness from the start of this fruitful period of the writing of the history
of women of the complexity of the task. That she was not alone in this
foresight is apparent from two volumes of essays on women's history which
were published in the early seventies. An influential volume appeared in
1974 under the title *Clio's Consciousness Raised*.[2] Mary Hartman's assertion
that 'Women's History is a field that is coming of age' in the preface to this
volume is justified by the fact that she identified many of the other issues
which women's historians would wrestle with for the rest of the century: the
place of feminism in women's history; how to make the history of women
part of the greater whole without becoming absorbed in a male perspective,
and the relationship of women's experience to the process of modernisation.
Hartman referred to women's history as a 'new research area' in which
interest had been stimulated by the emergence of social history and the
women's movement. She criticised feminists for being too inclined towards
the creation of heroines, the 'male oppression model' of explanation, and
applauded work which showed signs of 'combining the methods and insights
of social history with a heightened awareness of and concern about women'.[3]
The essays in the volume had all been presented as papers at the first of the
Berkshire Women's History Conference in 1973. These conferences developed very quickly into a focal point for and demonstration of 'the vigor of the
enterprise' in the USA: 600 historians attended the first Berkshire Conference,
and 2,000 came to the second one in 1974.[4] Hartman identified several
strands the papers had in common, among them a determination not to
'extract' women from history, and a reflection of current concerns about women
and women's roles. For Hartman 'Perhaps the most important question
that most of these articles provokes concerns the effects on the lives of
women of the changes broadly associated with modernisation.'[5] I shall return to this fruitful and long-running controversy later on in this chapter.

Two years after *Clio's Consciousness Raised*, Gerda Lerner's 1969 path-
breaking article was published, together with another, 'Placing women in
history: a 1975 perspective' in *Liberating Women's History*, edited by Berenice
Carroll.[6] Historians who were studying women were doing so with a defiant
self-consciousness which is apparent in this collection of articles, many of
them already published in journals in the early seventies. Several of the essays
reflected on the absence of women in history and identified the attitudes

which had led to this neglect. For some at least of the authors, the struggle to retrieve a history of women was part of a wider struggle against male supremacy.[7] But the nature of these contributions is a salutary warning against any assumptions we at the turn of the century might have about any lack of subtlety in the contribution to women's history of the women's movement of the late sixties and seventies. To make this clear, I will look in some detail at one chapter written by three American historians (Ann D. Gordon, Mary-Jo Buhle and Nancy Schrom Dye) which considered 'The problem of women's history', from an assertively feminist perspective, one which fully allowed for complexity and paradox. For these historians, feminism represented a challenge to 'society's organization of personal relations at the most intimate level of human experience', and located 'the lives of women, all women, at the center of efforts to comprehend and transform social structures'. For them, history was inextricably linked to their own 'efforts to transcend the imposition of contemporary institutions and values on our lives'.[8] But they also recognised that 'the past does not contain our vision; we haven't any model of liberation'.[9] They were aware that 'women's sisterhood has been affirmed with the ambivalent effect of raising new interest in the study of women *and* providing a new focus of potential confusion about women's caste-like condition'.[10]

The authors began with a review of the way history women had been seen as a timeless. They acknowledged the contribution made by social history where 'new advances in historical methodology coupled with feminist questions promise to expand our knowledge'.[11] They detected a dawning recognition of 'the relationship of women's movements to major social change in American Society'.[12] They identified the beginning of a process of revising notions of historical significance, 'to encompass personal, subjective experience as well as public and political activities'.[13] They stressed the need to avoid separating women's role in the workplace from her role in the family, and the need to avoid separating the lives of women from the wider social structures. One danger they warned against was 'the negativity of women's relationships with the larger society' becoming an exclusive focus, and they wanted to historicise the concept of oppression which 'meant different things to different groups and classes of women'.[14] On the same track, they sought to move the focus of women's history beyond the 'bond women share by virtue of their sex', arguing that the result of such a concentration did little to explain the dynamics of women's lives, or the conditions which underlie them. Moreover, it 'does violence to the lives of black women and men under slavery and side steps white women's role in that enslavement'.[15] Likewise, class might be 'received through men', but was nevertheless part of 'the condition of daily life, as real for women as for men'. In the past the categorisation of women as a separate caste had placed women outside history, and the analysis of women 'based on static concepts such as caste or oppressed group render history an external process, a force which presses against women's lives without reciprocal interaction'.[16]

This early article thus raised many of the themes which would dominate the debates among historians of gender for the next twenty years: the significance of the personal and the subjective; the agency of women in the process of social change, and the dangers of an exclusive focus on oppression and sisterhood. Like several other essays in the volume it was jointly written, a sign of the commitment of these historians of women to ideals of co-operative, non-competitive working. The content of the essays within this volume demonstrated the wide-ranging topics which historians of women were beginning to research and write. There were studies of gynaecology in seventeenth-century England; of the Women's Trade Union League at the turn of the century; of Feminism and Liberalism in Wilhelmine Germany, and the working and political experience of women in Weimar Germany; of social change in Iberian and Latin American cultures, and of women in convents in colonial Mexico; of male–female relations in Algeria; of the elusiveness of the experience of medieval women, and more general essays on 'Black womanhood' and 'Women, work and the social order'. The volume was an implicit statement of the diversity of women's historical experience: what was meant by the expression 'women' was raised explicitly at the end of their essay on 'Sex and class in colonial and nineteenth century America' by Ann. D. Gordon and Mary-Jo Buhle. They commented: 'There has been no single definition of woman, but rather a succession of definitions in which self-conscious feminism has been provoked, transformed or suppressed, and provoked again.'[17] This perspective, later to become central to debates between women historians, was put even more strongly by Sheila Ryan Johansson in her contribution to this volume, entitled '"Herstory" as History; A New Field or Another Fad?' She described how it had become apparent in her research into women and the law 'that women as women scarcely exist'. Women were defined by age, marital status and blood relations, and their legal status was 'further complicated by class distinctions, and sometimes by race and religion'.[18] She had become aware of the impossibility of generalisations across culture and period, the need for comparisons, and the inescapability of value judgements. She found that the status of women had varied over time, and not one phenomenon, whether it be Christianity or capitalism, is the original source of 'unfavourable status'.[19]

The final section of Johannson's article was entitled 'Beyond victimization: women as social agents'. In arguing for the ability of women to affect 'the structure, functioning and historical unfolding of their societies',

Johansson referred to Berenice Carroll's discussion of 'the powers of the "powerless"':

> Carroll argues that the allegedly 'powerless', i.e., those lacking the power of dominance or control over others, nevertheless exercise important forms of social power which, though difficult to mobilize in conscious, organized ways, are probably those forms of power on which all majority, long-term social change depends.[20]

Women's power and agency were, not unexpectedly, to be central concerns for historians of women throughout the period covered by this book. A sense of the power afforded by the study of history is apparent in Johanssonn's confident and optimistic essay which finished with the assertion that 'women cannot afford to lack a consciousness of a collective identity, one which necessarily involves a shared awareness of the past'.[21] This was a political statement and one which was also being declared on the other side of the Atlantic where a different development in the writing of the history of women was taking place.

One of the essays in the compilation put together by Carroll was by Juliet Mitchell, a New Zealander born in 1940 and living in London. Mitchell was not a historian: she did her undergraduate and postgraduate studies in English and subsequently became a lecturer in that discipline. The women's movement drew her into politics, and feminism into the study of Freud. The essay in Carroll's book was extracted from her study of women's oppression, *Woman's Estate*, published in the UK in 1971, and in the US in 1973. In it, she provided a neat and categorical model for 'women's condition throughout history'.[22] The model consisted of a structure formed by four key factors; 'production, reproduction, sexuality, and the socialization of children'.[23] She accepted that women's situation at any moment in history was 'a complex unity', nevertheless stated firmly that 'the variations of women's condition throughout history will be the result of different combinations of these elements', and that 'each independent sector . . . is ultimately . . . determined by the economic factor'.[24] She used Althusser's reconstruction of the Freudian concept of 'overdetermination' to describe the complexity of the way change in women's condition occurred.[25] As each of the four key factors which contributed to women's condition moved at a different pace, they were combined in different ways at different times. The contradictions which arose within the social structures as a result of these combinations sometimes reinforced one another and sometimes cancelled each other out.

Such a clear declaration of a theoretical stance was atypical of British historians, but it is apparent that the contributions to women's history in the UK in the seventies had their roots in a social history strongly influenced by Marxism. In 1976, Mitchell was co-editor with Ann Oakley, a sociologist, of *The Rights and Wrongs of Women*, a collection of essays from a variety of disciplines.[26] The subjects of the three essays on history reflected the influence of Marxist history: women's work in early nineteenth-century London, 'Women and nineteenth-century radical politics', and 'Women in American trade unions.' Sally Alexander's essay challenged the widely held perception by labour historians that women were insignificant operators outside the household. Feminist history, she asserted, had released from obscurity 'the wives, mothers and daughters of working men', not only as members of families, domestic workers, and mothers of the next generation but also as workers in the labour market. She judged that as a result it was necessary to rewrite 'the history of production itself', because from a feminist perspective it was a history of a struggle not only between worker and capitalist, but a history of 'the development of a particular form of the sexual division of labour in relation to that struggle'.[27] Her study revealed the extent of women's participation in the labour force not only in the 'slop and sweated trades', but in jobs which did not fit in easily with accepted definitions of '"the working-class"': needlewomen working at home, charwomen, prostitutes and thieves. In none of these occupations were wages sufficient to allow women to remain independent of men. So the survey also revealed 'the tenacity of the sexual division of labour'.[28] Dorothy Thompson's contribution to the volume was concerned with the political perspectives of working-class women in the early nineteenth century, a subject later fully studied by Barbara Taylor in a book described in Chapter Three. Thompson acknowledged the division between the aspirations of working and middle-class women in the 'women's emancipation movement' and then went on to trace the evidence of working-class women's participation in the political and social movement labelled as Chartism. At the end of the chapter she raised questions about the apparent decline in women's participation in radical politics from the 1840s. Possible answers seemed to lie in the changing nature of working-class politics into a more sophisticated and structured, but also less radical operation. But she also suggested that 'working-class women seem to have accepted an image of themselves which involved both home-centredness and inferiority. They could not, in the nature of their way of life, assume the decorative and useless role which wealthier classes imposed on women in this period, but they do seem to have accepted some of its implications'.[29]

The apparent shift in women's self-concept and behaviour in the first half of the nineteenth century would continue to fascinate historians on both sides of the Atlantic into eighties. In the early seventies, many of the issues which were to absorb the practitioners of women's history had been raised. Fierce debates were also stirring. The dispute among historians about the relative power of women before and after industrialization was sparking, although differences were still expressed within a powerful ideology of sisterhood which resonates with the female world of nineteenth century women. Barbara Sicherman asserted in a review essay published in 1975 that 'the single most important issue' with which historians of women were engaged was that of 'how women's status has changed with industrialization'.[30] Gerda Lerner had raised the question in 1969, and an article by Joan Scott and Louise Tilly suggested that the contrast between preindustrial and industrial patterns of work for women had been exaggerated: women continued to contribute to the family economy in a variety of ways well into the industrial era.[31]

In their introduction to *The Rights and Wrongs of Women*, Mitchell and Oakley had identified the feminist perspective of the contributors as a recognition of women 'as a distinct and oppressed social group'.[32] Yet a fair proportion of the introduction to *The Rights and Wrongs of Women* consisted in a challenge to the contemporary obsession with 'sisterhood'. The authors identified one of the consequences of that concept, 'the redefinition of the value and status of personal experience', and the ensuing analysis of women's oppression 'through the medium of accounts of private experiences'. From these studies had emerged what they called 'songs of glory', proclaiming hope of a more female-oriented society and provoking 'a search for a golden age of matriarchy in the past'.[33] The dangers which could come from extolling women's role in the private sphere would be the focus of an intense scrutiny by American historians of the nineteenth century at the end of the decade, and the spectre of the 'golden age' would haunt early modernist historians in the early nineties.

The British historian whose name is most closely associated with what she termed 'the rediscovery' of women's history in the 1970s is Sheila Rowbotham. She was part of a circle of friendship born of the women's movement which included Sally Alexander and Juliet Mitchell. She attended a Methodist school in Yorkshire from which she went as a student to Oxford in the early sixties. There she found it 'very difficult to study history which was not about Parliament and the growth of the treasury or about cabinets, treaties and coalitions, partly because we barely questioned how we should be taught and partly because a different kind of history was still in the making'.[34] The 'meekness' of the student population was 'particularly true of women, who were a tiny minority in a male stronghold and subtly taught our place by being told how privileged we were to be there at all.'[35] The 'other kind of history' which was 'shaping' she glimpsed in the person of Richard Cobb and in the work of Edward and Dorothy Thompson.[36] Their work was 'nurtured' by the Communist Party historians' group and the Worker's Educational Association and led to the Ruskin History Workshops which, in the late sixties, grew larger and larger. Implicit in this historical work informed by Marxism, and focusing on the struggles of the powerless, Rowbotham recognised 'the possibility of studying the position and action of women'. But it took the growth of 'women's liberation' to add 'the contours of the female historical experience'.[37]

For Rowbotham, there is an inextricable link between her commitment to women's history and to the women's movement. The idea of holding the first conference of the nascent British women's movement arose from a meeting of women at one of the Ruskin History Workshops. Sally Alexander later recalled that when the idea of a meeting of those who might be 'interested in working on "Women's History"'' was put to the Workshop it was greeted with laughter.[38] So it was with indignation and determination that Sheila Rowbotham, Sally Alexander and others began to look at their own past. Rowbotham fully recognised for the first time the extent of the neglect of women in history, and as a socialist she turned to the role women had played in socialist movements in the past for her first book, *Women, Resistance and Revolution* (1972). This was quickly followed by *Women's Consciousness, Man's World* (1973) which had grown out of the research for the earlier book. In it she described 'historical self-consciousness' as a 'tumultuous and wayward odyssey which for many of us has only just begun'.[39] Her next book, published in the same year, was an ambitious leap in that odyssey, covering '300 years of women's oppression and the fight against it'.[40] *Hidden from History* came, as the preface states, 'directly from a political movement'[41]: in the year after *Hidden from History* was published in the UK, there appeared in the US *Women in Modern America: A Brief History* by Lois Banner.[42] In her introduction, Banner wrote that social history and the 'new feminist movement' had 'coincided to stimulate studies about women'.[43] Rowbotham's 'political movement' was rather different from that of Banner in that it conflated feminism and socialism, both of which, she argued, raised questions about women's conditions in the past. In her book Rowbotham 'tried to explore both what has been specific to women as a sex and the manner in which class has cut across this oppression.' The central thread was an examination of 'Patriarchy, the power of men as a sex to dispose of women's capacity to labour, especially in the family', and her realisation that there was no direct and simple relationship between patriarchy and class exploitation.[44] In her research, she 'kept coming across many related questions which are also surfacing in the women's movement today'. She described a process whereby the women's movement was raising questions which led her to look for answers in a history of women, and in that history she found yet further questions. Moreover, she became aware of the knots which would be difficult to disentangle, and the delusive mirrors to be met on that journey. 'A critical culture' such as feminism, she saw as fragile, brittle, taut with the effort which has gone into its creation.[45]

Rowbotham has continued to write and publish prolifically, pursuing some of the leads she had opened up in *Hidden from History*: however, she has remained on the margins of academia. As Martha Vicinus put it in her introduction to a collection of essays published in 1972, 'The Women's Liberation Movement has brought back to life, if not academic respectability, the study of women.'[46] Vicinus was a Professor of English: another characteristic of women's history was that it was done by many who were not, by training at least, historians. Vicinus defined her work as 'women studies', and described the prevailing attitude to this 'new field' as 'widespread distrust'. This distrust was a compound of doubts about a lack of 'academic depth and rigor', whether there was enough material to study and the insistence that 'we must maintain our loyalty to a particular discipline lest we lose ourselves in an ill-defined area without "acceptable" criteria of research or clear academic standards.' But the most 'common criticism', wrote Vicinus, was the accusation that such research 'might be biased, trivial or, worst of all, trendy'.[47] Rowbotham had commented in the introduction to the American edition of *Hidden from History* that there was a dearth of studies of sexuality, maternity and 'production and reproduction in the household and the family'.[48] The subject matter of the essays in *Suffer and Be Still* included menstruation, prostitution, venereal disease and women's sexuality: clearly change was already taking place. The shift in focus to the domestic and the sexual was partly the result of the impact of anthropological studies on history, and in 1974 a volume of essays on anthropology appeared which was to prove influential in the thinking of women's historians.[49]

In the preface to *Women, Culture and Society*, Michelle Zimbalist Rosaldo and Louise Lamphere described the genesis of the book from the demands of a collective of female graduate students in anthropology at Stanford in 1971: the students organised an undergraduate lecture course, 'Women in cross-cultural perspective'. At more or less the same time anthropologists in other colleges and universities began to prepare similar courses, and to consider both what anthropologists might have to say about women and how an interest in women might provide a new perspective in their field. Appropriately, then, the stimulus for this work was coming from below, from students who, contrary to what the introduction to the book identified as the dominant ideology of their culture, found women's lives interesting. Rosaldo made the links between the academic study of women and their contemporary situation explicit in her essay: 'A theoretical overview'. Her perception was that women had attempted to achieve equality in modern societies by seeking 'grounds for female solidarity and opportunities for women in men's working world'. But she believed that 'as long as the domestic sphere remains female, women's societies, however powerful, will never be the political equivalent of men's', and that only an elite of women would be able to enter the public world. Her solution was to restructure the 'assymmetry between work and the home' by men's entry into the domestic sphere.[50]

Rosaldo and Lamphere summarised the contributors' findings as indicating that 'women's subordination', while universal, was various, and dependent on particular 'social and economic factors'; it was, they concluded in implicit agreement with the perspective of essayists in *Liberating Women's History*, 'a cultural product accessible to change'.[51] Their book raised issues which have remained crucial to women's historians: the genesis of women's oppression, whether it was indeed the result of economic and social forces, and the potential of women's own worlds to challenge that oppression would be the subject of debate for the next twenty-five years. The oppression of women was, of course, the issue which stimulated the women's movement of the seventies. The stimulus provided by the current experience of women historians is also apparent in one of the most vigorous of the research pursuits which was being undertaken in the seventies: the particular world of women, a world which historians had virtually ignored, but which those engaged in the women's movement increasingly valued.

Carroll Smith-Rosenberg was to become one of the best known of women's historians who focused on the world of women, and she had contributed an essay in *Clio's Conscousness Raised* entitled 'Puberty to menopause' which was later republished in a collection of her essays.[52] Most of the primary source material she used to 'examine Victorian American attitudes towards puberty and menopause in women' was the 'professional and popular writings of the medical profession'.[53] Only towards the end of the essay did she tentatively approach the question of how women viewed the menopause. This shift in her perspective was perhaps stimulated, and certainly accompanied by a move into the realm of psychology towards the end of the essay. Tempted, as she put it, 'to elaborate a psychological interpretation of these gynecological metaphors and formulations', she glanced briefly at Karen Horney's theory regarding male fear of woman as a pre-Oedipal phenomenon.[54] The use of insights provided by psychoanalysis would be a strong, if narrow thread in the writing of the history of women over the ensuing quarter-century.

Smith-Rosenberg had published an article jointly with her husband in 1973 in which they used 'normative descriptions of the female role' in order to analyse the relationships between social change and social stress.[55] The article looked at 'the ideological attack mounted by prestigious and traditionally minded men' on the growing number of women who were moving beyond the traditional role of mother and housekeeper.[56] Increasingly unsatisfied with the use of material from the male establishment to attempt to understand women's changing perceptions, Smith-Rosenberg turned to women's own voices as expressed in their private diaries and in their letters to each other. She had found a space in a new and rapidly widening landscape for historians. In 1975 she explored this landscape in 'The new woman and the new history'.[57] This essay, which is referred to in Chapter One, was written in response to a challenge to the validity of 'a special history of women'. In Smith-Rosenberg's view there was indeed a valid 'women's history', one that was 'forcing scholars to re-evaluate the canons of traditional historiography, to reconsider theories of causality and periodization, and to develop new sources and new modes of interpretation.' She joined together the 'New Social History' with women's history in their insistence that 'the most significant and intriguing historical questions relate to the events, the causal patterns, the pyschodynamics of private places'. This concern with the private had, in her view, led historians to reverse the usual assumptions about the causal process; they were now wondering whether developments in the private sphere 'may have causally affected' the public arena. In another article published in the same year, 1975, Smith-Rosenberg explored 'The female world of love and ritual: relations between women in nineteenth century America'.[58] There she found that female friendships were emotionally central to women's lives, and in the world created by such bonds, 'closeness, freedom of emotional expression, and uninhibited physical contact' were possible, in contrast often to the world where men and women mixed. In this world where men were excluded women were able to 'develop a sense of inner security and self-esteem', and they had status and power. She challenged the assumption that separation from men necessarily implied that such women were sub-ordinate to them. Nor did she see women to be necessarily isolated in the nuclear family since they formed and greatly valued and kinship and friendship ties.

This perspective was shared by Linda Gordon whose voice would be heard in many of the debates between women historians in the ensuing years. Gordon had contributed an essay to the collection in *Clio's Consciousness Raised* in which she examined the supporters of the 'voluntary motherhood' movement and found they were a disparate group which included suffragists, free lovers and purity reformers. They sought to change the double standard of sexuality by means of abstinence, rejecting mechanical means of birth control. Gordon shared Rowbotham's sense that her writing was informed by what she referred to as the 'divided, clumsy, contradictory, often pernicious mass women's movement' which had 'made me write this book'. Gordon wrote this in the introduction to *Women's Body, Women's Right*, which was published in the USA in 1976 and in the UK in 1977.[59] Indeed, the purpose of the book was 'to argue for my own view of the direction that feminism should take, and my understanding of its history underscores my certainty that I am right'.[60] Gordon's thesis was that 'reproductive freedom cannot be separated from the totality of women's freedom'. She also became convinced that despite the exploitation by those with power of social movements such as the struggle for the availability of the means for birth control, 'these manipulations are not part of an unending chain'; the chains of oppression could be broken.[61]

One of the most significant of the dimensions of women's history in the early seventies, and one that remained a focus for debate, was indeed its connection with feminism. Hilda Smith from the University of Maryland contributed an article to *Liberating Women's History* on 'Feminism and the methodology of women's history', in which she argued that it was 'necessary . . . to view the development of women's history from the feminist perspective of women as a sociological group'.[62] Her justification for this was that '[S]exual division has been one of the most basic distinctions within society encouraging one group to view its interests differently from another.' She had no problem in regarding 'women as a group' because they had 'held a particular position in society regardless of other restrictions on their lives'.[63] Her understanding of feminism – which, she acknowledged, was a concept which lacked 'exactitude' – was that it consisted in the view that women were a 'distinct sociological group for which there are established patterns of behaviour, special legal and legislative restrictions, and customarily defined roles', which were less fulfilling than those of men, and a belief that women were subject to a 'process of indoctrination from earliest childhood'.[64]

Hilda Smith's orderly understanding might not be acceptable to those historians of women who believed that it was not possible to provide a definition of women across time, and by others who asserted that women could find both power and fulfillment in a woman's culture. The seeds were being sown for a dispersal of women historians in different directions, a process foreseen and welcomed by Gerda Lerner in the second of her contributions to *Liberating Women's History*. This article was entitled 'Placing Women in History: a 1975 Perspective', and in it she reviewed 'the brief span of five years in which American historians have begun to develop women's history as an independent field'.[65] Looking back over the five years (which are those covered by this chapter), Lerner provided a lucid overview of the essential nodes of the project which had begun with such vigour in that period. She identified precisely the points of departure for a rich and complex practice of women's history. Looking at what she referred to as 'compensatory history' she emphasised the need to recognise differences between women's and men's experiences in order 'to comprehend the full complexity of society at a given stage of its development . . . .'.[66] There was need, then, for 'contribution history' in which women's contributions to the whole of society and not just to other women would be studied. Lerner agreed with Hilda Smith that women were indoctrinated in the male value system: 'The decisive historical fact about women is that the *areas* of their functioning, not only their status *within* those areas, have been determined by men.' She emphasised both the significance and the endurance of women's 'subjection' which had, she asserted, antedated other oppressions and outlasted them.[67] Yet in her view 'the ongoing and continuing contribution of women to the development of human culture cannot be found by treating them only as victims of oppression . . .'.[68] For her, '[T]he true history of women is their ongoing function in that male-defined world, *on their own terms.*' Lerner made reference in the essay to the ways in which this work was already going forward as historians were showing how it was possible 'to approach the same material and interpret it from a new perspective'. In particular, they were making distinctions 'between prescription and behaviour, between myth and reality'. The detailed analysis of the Victorian ideal of women's behaviour by Barbara Welter had revealed that the concern of the prescriptive writers with 'women's domesticity was, in fact, a response to the opposite trend in society'.[69] She also noted that Joan Kelly was challenging the male domination implicit in periodisation. However, the problem remained that it was hard to avoid using a male value system when trying 'to fit women's past into the empty spaces of historical scholarship'.[70]

As Barbara Sicherman noted, the enterprise of women's history in the early seventies was vigorous, and scholarly work was 'accumulating at a rapid rate'.[71] But, she added, 'historians, long immersed in their primary sources' had begun 'to search for larger meanings. They have not yet found them. There is currently no consensus on an appropriate conceptual framework for women's history; few historians of the American experience – Gerda Lerner is the exception – have even addressed themselves to the issues.' Historians of women were, however, beginning the search for a methodological framework. Lerner and Sicherman both referred to the Marxism which informed the work of Mitchell and Rowbotham, and to Mitchell's inclusion of sexuality in the concept of production. As expressed in her 1975 article, Lerner's view was that unless changes in production and reproduction 'are accompanied by changes in consciousness, which in turn results in institutional change, they do not favourably affect the lives of women'.[72] Consciousness for Lerner was vital. Earlier in the article she had argued that in the nineteenth century, as women became aware of the 'separate interests of women as a group . . . so did their consciousness become woman-defined'.[73] So historians could move from work on data to female sources and to the study of female consciousness – here she refers to the work of Smith-Rosenberg. Smith-Rosenberg had described her interpretation of female friendships as 'cultural or psychosocial', but her exploration had taken her into psychoanalytical territory, a domain in which she had placed a wary foot in 'Puberty to menopause'. In her historiographical essay, Smith-Rosenberg recommended combining the 'analytic models' of ethnohistory and psychological history.[74] The former model, borrowed from anthropology and sociology, would 'provide a way of placing individual experience over a lifetime within a social framework. Demographic material would be placed alongside prescriptive literature and actual behavior reported in diaries and letters.'[75] But this model would not 'provide us with tools sufficient to analyse the experiential quality of life'; for this the historian should turn to the 'infrapsychic focus of psychological theory'.[76] She was well aware of the difficulty of finding appropriate material for a study of the experiential nature of the lives of working-class women, and she referred to this problem as one of the divisions which had arisen among historians of women. But she asserted at the end of the essay that there were common determinants in the lives of women: economic and demographic structures; cultural belief systems; the internal dynamics of the family and basic human psychological needs.

The strikingly ambitious nature of the new enterprise of women's history is clear from this article, and it offers a powerful image of women struggling with an immense and diverse task. Both British and American historians of women were clearly well aware in the early seventies that their 'subject' was 'complex . . . full of paradoxes which elude precise definitions and defy synthesis'.[77] Historians from both sides of the Atlantic were fully aware of how difficult it is, as Lerner put it, 'to conceptualize women as a group, since they are dispersed throughout the population'.[78] Sheila Rowbotham foresaw, nevertheless, that a study of 'the material circumstances of women's lives' would lead to a new perspective on the historical understanding of men as well as women.[79] In the mid-seventies women's history was an open and liberating field of endeavour. Historians were choosing individual paths, and it is difficult to provide a clear map of the choices made. A comparison between Smith-Rosenberg's 1975 essay with one which was published ten years later encapsulates one of the problems with attempting to reconstruct the history of women's history. Writing later, Smith-Rosenberg described the early trajectory of women's historians in linear terms. Their first inspiration was political, she stated categorically. Ten years earlier she had acknowledged that the contemporary women's movement had reinforced a trend, but she traced the beginnings of women's history to the 'suggestive implications' of research on women's lives undertaken by 'a few historians of women'.[80] The references she provided for her later essay were all published in the 1980s. The world of women's history was moving so fast that those engaged in it can be excused for giving every appearance of giddiness. It was perhaps the sense of turbulence, or at least of disorder in their world which led historians of women to grasp at the concept of gender as a means of providing order and coherence to their work.

Notes and references

1. Gerda Lerner, 'New approaches to the study of women in American history', *Journal of Social History*, 3:1 (1969), pp. 53–62.

2. Mary Hartman and Lois Banner, eds., *Clio's Consciousness Raised: New Perspectives on the History of Women* (New York, 1974).

3. Ibid., pp. xii, vii.

4. Barbara Sicherman, 'American history', *Signs*, 1:1 (Winter 1975), pp. 461–5.

5. Hartman and Banner (1974), p. xii.

6. Berenice Carroll, ed., *Liberating Women's History: Theoretical and Critical Essays* (Chicago, 1976). Gerda Lerner, 'Placing women in history', *Feminist Studies*, 3 (1978), pp. 5–15.

7. Carroll, ed. (1976), p. 71.

8. Ibid., p. 84.

9. Ibid., p. 85.

10. Ibid., p. 89.

11. Ibid., p. 81.

12. Ibid., p. 82.

13. Ibid., p. 89.

14. Ibid., pp. 86–7.

15. Ibid., p. 87.

16. Ibid., p. 89.

17. Ibid., p. 293.

18. Ibid., p. 404.

19. Ibid., p. 410.

20. Ibid., pp. 416–17.

21. Ibid., p. 427.

22. Ibid., p. 396.

23. Ibid., p. 385.

24. Ibid., p. 396.

25. Ibid., p. 385.

26. Anne Oakley and Juliet Mitchell, eds., *The Rights and Wrongs of Women* (London, 1976).

27. Sally Alexander, 'Women's work in nineteenth-century London: a study of the years 1820–50', in ibid., pp. 59–60.

28. Ibid., pp. 110–11.

29. Dorothy Thompson, 'Women and nineteenth-century Radical politics: a lost dimension', in ibid., pp. 137–8.

30. Barbara Sicherman (1975), p. 463.

31. Joan Wallach Scott and Louise Tilly, 'Women's work and the family in nineteenth-century Europe', *Comparative Studies in Society and History*, 17 (January, 1975).

32. Oakley and Mitchell (1976), p. 9.

33. Ibid., p. 11.

34. Sheila Rowbotham, *Dreams and Dilemmas* (London, 1983), p. 170.

35. Ibid.

36. Ibid., p. 171.

37. Ibid., p. 172.

38. Sally Alexander, 'Women, class and sexual differences in the 1830s and 1840s: some reflections on the writing of a feminist history', *History Workshop Journal*, 17 (Spring, 1984), pp. 125–149.

39. Sheila Rowbotham, *Woman's Consciousness, Man's World* (London, 1973), p. 28.

40. Sheila Rowbotham, *Hidden from History* (London, 1973).

41. Ibid., p. lx.

42. Lois Banner, *Women in Modern America: A Brief History* (New York, 1974).

43. Ibid., p. v.

44. Rowbotham (1973), p. vix.

45. Rowbotham (1983), p. 174.

46. Martha Vicinus, ed., *Suffer and Be Still: Women in the Victorian Age* (Indiana, 1972), p. vii.

47. Ibid., p. viii.

48. Rowbotham (1983), p. 181.

49. Michelle Zimbalist Rosaldo and Louise Lamphere, eds., *Women, Culture and Society* (Stanford, 1974).

50. Ibid., p. 42.

51. Ibid., p. 13.

52. Carroll Smith-Rosenberg, *Disorderly Conduct: Visions of Gender in Victorian America* (Oxford, 1985).

53. Ibid., p. 182.

54. Ibid., p. 196.

55. Carroll and Charles Smith-Rosenberg, 'The female animal: medical and biological views of woman and her role in nineteenth-century America', *Journal of American History*, LX (September, 1973), pp. 332–56.

56. Ibid., p. 333.

57. Carroll Smith-Rosenberg, 'The new woman and the new history', *Feminist Studies*, 3 (Autumn, 1975a), pp. 185–98.

58. Carroll Smith-Rosenberg, 'The female world of love and ritual', *Signs*, 1:3 (Autumn 1975b), pp. 1–29.

59. Linda Gordon, *Woman's Body, Woman's Right* (New York, 1976; London, 1977).

60. Ibid., p. xviii.

61. Ibid., p. 418.

62. Carroll, ed. (1976), p. 369.

63. Ibid.

64. Ibid., p. 370.

65. Ibid., p. 357.

66. Ibid.

67. Ibid., p. 361.

68. Ibid., p. 358.

69. Ibid., p. 359.

70. Ibid., p. 360.

71. Sicherman (1975), p. 462.

72. Lerner (1975), p. 12.

73. Ibid., pp. 5–6.

74. Smith-Rosenberg (1975a), p. 192.

75. Ibid., p. 193.

76. Ibid., p. 195.

77. Lerner (1969), pp. 56–7.

78. Ibid., p. 56.

79. Rowbotham (1983), p. 179.

80. Smith-Rosenberg (1975a), p. 187.

CHAPTER THREE

Liberating women's history 1976–83

In her introduction to the American edition of *Hidden from History*, Sheila Rowbotham had written that 'feminism is not enough to encompass theoretically the forms of oppression women have shared with men . . . The fate of all women has not been the same'.[1] British historians in the seventies placed an increasing emphasis on women's diversity within a continued insistence on a common oppression. On the other side of the Atlantic, women's history broadened out very rapidly and the conviction that history as a discipline was changing as a result of the presence of women was confidently expressed in the writings of historians. In this chapter I will look first at increasing complexity of the task facing historians of women in the United States, and the resulting debates about what conceptual framework was appropriate to their work. The concept of patriarchy was at the centre of one such debate, and British historians shared in this deliberation. Increasingly, a focus on gender in the study of historical material was put forward as a way of making such work coherent, and also of challenging accepted ways of seeing the past, one which could encompass both women's and men's histories. Discussions about theoretical frameworks were accompanied by the discomfort of containing divergent judgements within the sisterhood of historians of women, an uneasiness which emerged at the end of the decade of the seventies in the debate on the nature and political potential of 'women's culture'. In Britain historians of women continued to assert the validity of their project, and links were made between their work and those of American historians. On either side of the Atlantic, the psychoanalytical understandings were drawn on to inform the study of history.

In the early summer of 1976 three highly significant articles putting forward the claims of historians of women that their discipline could and should change the landscape of the writing of history were published in

American journals. In May 'women's evolving role in America' was 'explored from several perspectives' in the journal *Current History*. The first perspective was that of Gerda Lerner who contributed an article entitled 'The majority finds its past'.[2] The bold opening paragraph of this article encapsulated the assertions of women's historians of the mid-seventies: that at least half of the world's experience was that of women, so that 'to write the history of women means documenting all of history'. The problem lay in the fact that this experience had been 'shaped for us through a value system defined by men' so that there was a task to be done in reconstructing 'the female experience: the history of women'. The work that had been completed on the retrieval of 'women worthies' from obscurity must be followed by a recognition of difference between women's experiences. 'The central question raised by women's history is: what would history be like if it were seen through the eyes of women and ordered by values they define.' Lerner called for more studies of women's political contribution through their own communities built on 'their own female culture' to supplement the history of women's struggle for the ballot. Implicit in this last point is the idea that women had indeed contributed to the political structures through their own separate culture: this issue would be debated in print with some vehemence four years later.

Nathalie Zemon Davis had been publishing work on the early modern history of France for ten years when she contributed a paper to the Second Berkshire Conference on the History of Women in October 1975 which was published as an article in *Feminist Studies* in the following year, entitled 'Women's history in transition'.[3] There she looked in some detail at two books which she judged to be the 'best products' of a period when there was a growing perception that 'the institution of the family and the relations between the sexes should not be perceived as essentially unchanging features of the European past'. The two books were Alice Clark's *Working Life of Women in the Seventeenth Century* and *La femme et le féminisme en France avant la Révolution* (1923) by Leon Abensour. As I have described in Chapter One, Zemon Davis pointed to many parallels between the experience and the practice of these early twentieth-century authors and the writers of women's history of the seventies, in particular the use of demography as a tool; the statistical work done on household size, and the attention paid to 'sexual or erotic activity'. She also declared that 'our goals are or should be more general and more sweeping than theirs'. Although she recognised that 'it is no more true today than in the nineteenth century that all practitioners of women's history have the same political hopes', and that both generations of women's historians wrote mainly about women, she advocated an interest in the history of both women and men. She held the goal of women's historians to be a new one: the understanding of 'the significance of the *sexes*,

41

of gender groups in the historical past'. It should become 'second nature for the historian, whatever her or his speciality, to consider the consequences of gender as readily, say, as those of class'. Such an approach would make it necessary for historians to rethink the central issues of 'power, social structures, property, symbols, and periodization'. Undertaking gender history, the relations between the sexes, could lead to the re-writing of all history, a project Gerda Lerner advocated. Zemon Davis also agreed with Lerner that the nature of power was 'a trickier business' than when the focus of historians had been largely on institutions, and believed that it needed to be 'examined in its full complexity'. She asked for a more complex model of social structure to be used. Notions of property had, in her view, been extended by the study of gender groups which revealed a new good – 'sex – ordinarily property and exchange in women'. These revelations had led to the raising of as yet unanswered questions concerning the ways in which this exchange functioned. The connection between symbols and actual behaviour is another complex problem to which Zemon Davis suggested possible answers. Referring to the richness of sexual symbolism, she wrote: 'I would expect to find that some of these symbols could be used not merely to keep women down and men up, women in and men outside, but could be twisted around to as to threaten the lines between these places and justify behaviour of a disorderly sort.' While welcoming the challenge to conventional conclusions in history, Zemon Davis was also cautious, calling for alternative hypotheses as a basis for more research, and warning of the need to 'distinguish speculation from generalization'. She was aware that the field of research envisaged by women's historians was opening up immense vistas.

The third important article published in 1976 was written by Joan Kelly.[4] Kelly was teaching at Sarah Lawrence College when a request from Gerda Lerner, followed by some forceful persuasion to develop a course of lectures about women in her field, had turned her ideas about the Renaissance completely upside down. Her rejection of the widely held notion of the equality of men and women in the Renaissance was to lead to her challenge to traditional periodisation.[5] In the *Signs* article Kelly put forward her perspective on the implications of women's history for the study of history in general. She dealt first with periodisation, arguing that the effect of examining periods of history in terms of their significance for the 'status' of women – which she defined as their 'roles and positions in society' – was to detect a pattern of loss of status for women in precisely the periods seen as witnessing 'progressive change'. What Kelly found most 'promising about the way periodization has begun to function in women's history' was that the history of men was being related to the history of women. Quoting Zemon Davis's identification of the understanding of 'the significance of the *sexes*, of gender groups in the historical past' as a goal for women's historians, Kelly held that the 'activity, power, and cultural evaluation of women' could only be assessed in relation to both the parallel aspects of men's history and 'the institutions and social developments that shape the social order'. The final section of Kelly's article put forward a theory of social change which traced the origins and historical forms of patriarchy to 'the society's mode of production'.

Patriarchy had been an obvious paradigm for the work of historians of women, and the concept had been implicit in the writing of British historians such as Sally Alexander. In her article on women's work in the nineteenth century described in the last chapter, Alexander identified the operation of the patriarchy – without naming it as such – in the sexual division of labour, whose origins she understood to lie in the family.[6] Sheila Rowbotham, however, became uncomfortable with the increasing use of this concept, a discomfort she investigated in an article published in 1979: 'The Trouble with Patriarchy'.[7] She believed that the application of this concept to the structure of women's history had arisen from a growing awareness that current Marxist ideas did not offer a sufficiently wide understanding of power relationships and hierarchy. While recognising the pertinence of this position Rowbotham held that patriarchy was too static a structure to encapsulate 'the kaleidoscope of forms within which women and men have encountered one another'. Her understanding of the word was that it emphasised biological difference and thus placed the emphasis on sexual difference rather than 'the social inequalities of gender – the different kinds of power societies have given to sexual differences, and the hierarchical forms these have imposed on human relationships'. Moreover, she asserted that the relationship between men and women has not been invariably antagonistic, as implied by the concept of patriarchy. In a reply to Rowbotham, Barbara Taylor and Sally Alexander defended the use of the concept patriarchy on the basis of the need for a theoretical underpinning to their 'research into women's lives and experience'.[8] In their view, 'History only answers questions which are put to it: without a framework for these questions we shall founder in a welter of dissociated and contradictory "facts".' Acknowledging a particular debt to Juliet Mitchell's writings, they wrote that they had found the tools they needed for a 'theory of gender' in feminist readings of anthropology and psychoanalysis. Whether they had read Joan Kelly's article advocating a 'doubled vision' which is described below is unclear, but their wariness of 'any attempt to "marry" the concepts of sex and class' is firmly stated: it might do for a theory of sex what marriage did for women, 'dissolve them into the stronger side of the partnership'. However, Michelle Rosaldo, who had edited the influential collection of essays *Women and Culture*, warned of 'The use and abuse of anthropology' by those searching for the origins of women's oppression.[9] She wrote that it seemed 'likely to me that sexual asymmetry can be discovered in all human social groups', but that attempting to find its source inevitably contained within it an acceptance of a dichotomous difference. Rosaldo joined Sheila Rowbotham in suggesting that such a notion of human beings reflected a lack of understanding that 'the individuals who create social relationships and bonds are themselves social creations'. Gender inequalities, she argued, were universal neither in their content nor their implications, and the roles played by men and women were shaped by other inequalities in the social world. Such inequalities could therefore only be 'intelligible in their locally specific terms'.

The need or desire for a theoretical framework seemed to be at variance with attentiveness to the complexity of the history of women. Joan Kelly, who had suggested that the origins and historical forms of patriarchy were linked to forms of production, attempted to resolve this tension in an article in which she identified a 'theoretical outlook' which she saw 'emerging out of the several schools and strands of feminist thought and scholarship'.[10] This outlook made possible a 'unified "doubled" view of the social order, and it promises to overcome certain conflicts in theory and practice that stem from earlier notions of sex oppression and social change'. She consolidated earlier threads in the writing of women's history into two main strands. The first had developed from a Marxist tradition and focused on the way the organisation of work outside the home obscured the work done by women and kept them dependent on men. The second strand grew from the work of radical feminists who had analysed the 'psychic, sexual, and ideological structures that differentiate the sexes, setting up an antagonistic relation of dominance and subjection between them'. Kelly sought to knit these strands back together. In her view, the separation between them had its origins in the 'nineteenth century conception of two sociosexual spheres'. She perceived feminist thought moving beyond the view of 'two spheres of social reality' to an awareness that what they saw were 'two (or three) sets of social relations': work and sex. Overcoming the former dualistic approach would, Kelly believed, allow for 'a sharpened sense of particularity', an awareness of the different ways women experienced sex oppression. It would also enable feminists to 'understand better the persistence of patriarchy'. The strength of patriarchy had lain in its ability 'in all its historical forms to assimilate itself so perfectly to socioeconomic, political, and cultural structures as to be virtually invisible'. The new doubled vision of feminism was making it possible to see both the operation of the 'sexual/reproductive' and the 'economic productive/reproductive' sets of relations operating. As a result it was now feasible not only to 'see how the patriarchal system works, but also to act with that vision – so as to put an end to it'.

Gerda Lerner shared Kelly's conviction that 'patriarchy as a system is historical: it has a beginning in history. If that is so, it can be ended by historical process'.[11] She spent eight years in the late seventies and early eighties 'working in the history of ancient Mesopotamia in order to answer the questions I consider essential to creating a feminist theory of history'. There she found that the search for the origin of patriarchy was 'far less significant than questions about the historical process by which patriarchy becomes established and institutionalized'.[12] In an article in the 1978 edition of *Feminist Studies* which concentrated on women's history, Lerner again called for a move beyond 'contribution history' towards a more integrated approach which would add gender to the concepts of class, race and ethnicity, and one which challenged traditional ideas about periodisation.[13] But she added that she had come to believe by then that such a 'new history' could not be fitted into any 'single methodology or framework', because of the 'complexities of the historical experience of all women'. It was not necessary, in Lerner's view, to have such a framework in order to achieve 'a paradigm shift . . . a fundamental re-evaluation of the assumptions and methodology of traditional history and traditional thought'.[14] This bold claim was made in a collection of Lerner's writings on women's history to date published in 1979. In the final chapter of *The Majority Finds Its Past* she identified the nature of 'The challenge of women's history' and returned to the themes which she had been developing over the past decade. At the heart of her thinking lay the notion of women's history as in itself providing 'a conceptual model and a strategy by which to focus on and isolate that which traditional history has obscured'.[15] Part of that conceptual model was the use of gender as an analytical category. She repeated her confident statement that the impact of such an approach would mean a redefinition of categories and values, and a shift in traditional periodisation.

Writing in the seventies reflects a sense among historians of women that the were, as Gerda Lerner put it, 'an embattled lot'.[16] The enemy was on the outside, and within the fold Lerner and her contemporaries were 'vitally interested in and involved in each other's work, trying to combat within ourselves and one another the competitiveness which is structured into our institutional and professional life and to substitute for it a new and as yet untested model of supportive and engaged scholarship'.[17] When advocating that the 'field of women's history' be an 'open forum', Nathalie Zemon Davis wondered whether this territory might become a 'battlefield'.[18] Recalling the publication of her article 'The female world of love and ritual', Smith-Rosenberg described it as assuming 'a life of its own'.[19] She clearly had a sense that it had been misjudged and misread by some historians whom she does not specify. The commitment to co-operation and the renunciation of competitiveness among historians of women was tested in a debate about the connections between the nineteenth-century world of women and the politics of the women's movement.

Perhaps the most substantial study of the woman's sphere which came out in the second half of the seventies was Nancy Cott's *The Bonds of Womanhood*. Cott wrote very much as a traditional historian, without reference to the feminist political context from which she was operating.[20] She focused on the 1830s which she saw as a 'turning point in women's economic participation, public activities, and social visibility'.[21] Women's political incapacity was made conspicuous by the granting of manhood suffrage, and their 'second-class position in the economy was thrown into relief' by the diversification of the agricultural base, and the growth in wage-earning. Women went where they could: they were recruited into textile factories; they 'pursued the one profession open to them, primary school teaching', and they took part in 'a variety of reform movements'.[22] Yet, at the same time, 'an emphatic sentence of domesticity was pronounced on women'.[23] There took place in that decade a debate between 'two seemingly contradictory visions of women's relation to society'.[24] One was the ideology of domesticity which envisaged women as limited to a role primarily in the home, and the other was feminism, which sought to remove constraints on the scope of women's activities.

Cott had originally intended to find out how the assembly of social attitudes later referred to by historians as the 'cult of true womanhood' (so named by Barbara Welter), and the 'cult of domesticity' (Cott cited an article published in 1964 by William Taylor as the first to use the term domesticity in this sense) related to the actual experiences of women. These attitudes were expressed in a literature of popular didactic writings which both 'glorified the home and women's role in it', and prescribed women's behaviour in the home.[25] Accepting the view that such writings addressed readers who were already convinced, Cott decided to look at the roots of such attitudes. She wanted to move beyond what was written about women to women's lives, so, like Smith-Rosenberg, she turned to personal documents. Indeed, at the end of the book, Cott associated different interpretations of the 'woman's sphere' by feminist historians with the different type of sources used. Didactic literature led to the interpretation of women as 'victims, or prisoners, of an ideology of domesticity that was imposed on them'. The published writings of women authors led to the observation that women 'made use of the ideology of domesticity for their own purposes', while those historians who relied on women's personal documents evaluated woman's sphere as 'the basis for a subculture among women that formed a source of strength and identity'.[26] Cott acknowledged her debt to these interpretations and then sought to free herself from 'the intrusion of mid-twentieth-century assumptions' about the limits of domesticity in drawing her conclusions.[27] Women's support for each other and their construction of a female value system which Smith-Rosenberg had also noted, became, in Cott's view, the source of a 'new kind of group consciousness, one which could develop into political consciousness. The "woman question" and the women's rights movement of the nineteenth century were predicated on the appearance of women as a discrete class and on the concomitant group-consciousness of sisterhood'.[28] Cott contended that nineteenth-century women, unlike contemporary feminists, saw no 'antithesis between women's obligations in the domestic realm and their general progress'.[29] The woman's sphere accommodated 'a range of specific choices for venturesome women so long as they subsumed these under the rubric of *female* duties . . .'.[30] Cott's conclusions thus provided a theoretical structure for the development of feminism from the 'bonds of womanhood'.

I have described Cott's work in some detail because the result of her research and her thinking was to put together two perspectives on women in early nineteenth-century America into a satisfying hypothesis concerning the process of change which saw women the agents, not victims. She had done as Lerner advocated in tracing the roots of a political feminism to women's own cultures. However, this linking of women's worlds with the politics of feminism does not seem to have satisfied some of Cott's contemporaries, although the desire to undertake supportive and engaged scholarship is apparent in the contributions to a symposium on 'Politics and culture in women's history' published in 1980 in *Feminist Studies*. In her introduction to the contributions, Judith Walkowitz expressed the hope that the symposium would 'serve to clarify the concept of women's culture and assess its political and theoretical significance'.[31] The debate was initiated by a provocative contribution from Ellen Dubois. Dubois's challenge to those who were focusing on women's culture had been identified by Barbara Sicherman in 1975. Indeed, Sicherman herself had raised the question of whether the pendulum had swung too far. 'Having left behind a model based exclusively on oppression, historians may be in danger of swinging to the opposite extreme and sentimentalizing women's experience. Women unquestionably succeeded in extending their sphere, but those who tried to go beyond it soon discovered its potency'.[32]

Dubois opened her essay with the dual affirmation that 'a feminist perspective is necessary to make women's history a vital intellectual endeavour, and women's history should give special attention to the history of the feminist movement'. The feminist conception of women's history, for Dubois, was that the 'central themes of women's experience' were 'oppression and the effort to understand and overcome it'.[33] She referred among other discoveries by women's historians to evidence for the existence of 'a very widespread, largely inchoate feminist consciousness among nineteenth century women'. Turning to what she referred to as the most 'significant theoretical formulation coming from these discoveries', that of 'women's culture', she raised questions about its relationship to feminism. Dubois noted Nancy Cott's identification of the 'development of women's consciousness of themselves as a group' as 'a necessary prerequisite for the emergence of a feminist movement', and pointed out that Cott herself warned that the feminism was not a direct and simple development from a women's culture. Indeed, Dubois's own research was suggesting to her that 'woman's rights feminism grew out of a critique of what we are calling women's culture'. She then moved on to criticise what she designated the 'dominant tendency in the study of women's culture' which was 'to look at it in isolation and to romanticize what it meant for women', and identified Carroll Smith-Rosenberg's writings as an example of this tendency. Dubois was anxious that the 'impulse that led us into women's history' would be satisfied by the discovery of the 'humanity and historical activity' of those who lived within a women's culture, so that the enquiry into the system which 'structured women's historical activity and shaped their oppression' would be forestalled. To avoid this outcome, Dubois called for adequate attention to be given to political questions, and the retention of a focus on social change. The thesis she had developed in her own study of *Feminism and Suffrage* had been that the demand for the vote 'required an active social movement to give it meaning and make it real', and that the demand had indeed generated 'a movement of increasing strength and vitality' which transformed the consciousness of women.[34] But for Dubois, sisterhood was not enough: feminism involved a politics which challenges the institutions of patriarchal power. These challenges may arise from a sense of collective sisterhood, but they do not arise automatically from this consciousness and they involve a shared set of ideas about how to change the political structures, and an organisation of efforts to effect such a change.

Carroll Smith-Rosenberg's response to Ellen Dubois reads as an angry retort.[35] She started with the accusation that Dubois's article 'espouses a revisionist history that would focus upon political issues and elite cadres of activists'. By implication Smith-Rosenberg agreed with Dubois that a focus on feminism legitimates and makes fruitful the study of women's history, but disagreed on three grounds with her own reconstruction of Dubois's argument. She interpreted Dubois as suspicious of the 'experience of the average woman'; asserting 'the causal centrality of the political', and ignoring 'the economic, demographic, and institutional factors that helped shape the political'. She understood Dubois's view to be that women's culture was 'dialectically opposed to feminism'. Her interpretation of Dubois's discussion of the connection between women's culture – a term which Smith-Rosenberg denied using – and feminism is that the former 'will generate neither a sense of female solidarity and strength nor a radical critique of society. Rather such female interaction will encourage conservative collaboration with the dominant male power system. This is Dubois's real message'. Smith-Rosenberg constructed a powerful metaphor from what she read into Dubois's article of the danger of women historians 'becoming modern Narcissae and, like the unicorn, entrapped by the impassioned contemplation of ourselves'. The crux of their difference was picked out by Smith-Rosenberg towards the end of her essay, when she quoted Dubois's assertion that ' "the pressing historical questions about women's culture" ' centred ' "on its relationship to feminism" '. Her own view was that 'the pressing questions about feminism centre on its relation to the existence of a female world'. For her, the root from which women could move towards feminism was one where they identified themselves as women, and a female community provided rich soil for such roots.

Two of the questions raised by the debate Smith-Rosenberg described as 'fascinating and complex' were those concerned with the boundaries between women's separate sphere and the wider society. What were the relationships between the 'values, rituals, and symbols women expressed among themselves and those of the larger society to which they also gave allegiance? How is power distributed within a segregated female world and how does this distribution reflect power relations between men and women?'. In her response to what she acknowledged was Dubois's 'strong case against historians who limit their studies to women's culture alone', Mary Jo Buhle agreed that women's culture could not be studied in isolation, but asserted that it was also the case that 'only through a study of women's culture can we assess nineteenth-century feminist consciousness and activity within its social context'.[36] The leaders of the postbellum women's movement 'spoke directly to the values' described by historians of women's culture, and it was not possible for historians to 'judge this political expression unless we understand the culture from which it sprang'. Gerda Lerner's response to Dubois also asserted that 'Woman's culture is the ground upon which women stand in their resistance to patriarchal dominance and their assertion of their own creativity in shaping society.'[37] But she added that whether women standing on such ground always resisted or sometimes reinforced the modes of class and gender domination would be a moot point in women's history for some years. Lerner's response was predicated on the need she perceived for keeping 'clean and sharp' those 'tools' of the struggle for 'intellectual emancipation'; the 'terms of our discourse and definitions'. She focused on Dubois's use of the terms 'feminism', and 'woman's culture' (in print at least, Dubois used the plural, women's culture; a significant difference). Lerner divided feminism into the concern with women's rights, which sought 'equal participation for women in the status quo', and the striving for emancipation, by which she meant the attainment of 'freedom from oppressive restrictions imposed by sex; self-determination; autonomy'. Accusing Dubois of using 'the term "woman's culture" as though is were meant to define "woman's sphere"', Lerner construed the expression as 'women's definition in their own terms', a definition that implied 'an assertion of equality and an awareness of sisterhood, the communality of women'.

The debate on women's culture and politics was linked in with another and older concept widely used by historians, that of class. In her contribution Temma Kaplan argued that a class analysis of the places where women were to be found illuminated women's lives in a way that focusing solely on either women's culture or on feminism did not.[38] A review article in the issue of *Feminist Studies* in which the debate on women's culture and politics had appeared linked Dubois's book with one published in Britain where class was a significant issue; the study of working-class suffragists from Lancashire, *One Hand Tied Behind Us*.[39] The reviewer, Christine Stansell, saw these two books as 'important attempts to integrate the study of politics and ideology, traditional concerns of male-dominated history, with the new women's history of the 1970s'. Both books raised 'important problems and perplexities about the nature of feminist radicalism'. Stansell was clearly committed to challenging male paradigms, and at the same time was fascinated by the separate development of a particular history of women. In the seventies, this fascination was more characteristic of American than British historians, as is indicated by a comparison between *One Hand Tied Behind Us* and a book by Judith Walkowitz, *Prostitution and Victorian Society: Women, Class and the State* published in the same year, 1978.[40] Both these studies challenged assumptions about British women's experience and agency within Victorian and Edwardian politics but the focus of the two books is very different. Walkowitz had begun her research in 1970 at a time when sexuality and prostitution were visibly emerging as legitimate subjects for historians. One chapter in *Suffer and Be Still* (Vicinus, 1972) had examined Victorian prostitution and the Contagious Diseases Acts which were to be focus of Walkowitz's book, but the perspective of the earlier study was very much that of social history. Walkowitz agreed that the Acts provided 'insight into important social and political developments in the mid-Victorian period', but she placed her study alongside the challenge to the concept of women as subordinated and silent victims made by Smith-Rosenberg, Mary Ryan and Linda Gordon. It was, Walkowitz declared, 'one chapter in the story of women's resistance to the dominant forces in society . . .'. She saw the wealth of material connected to the Acts and the struggle for their repeal as an opportunity to study class and gender relations. She took as the starting point of her analysis the argument of Michel Foucault that the 'obsessive preoccupation with and codification of sex' in Victorian society was a method of facilitating 'control of an ever-widening circle of human activity': it was an exercise of power.[41] The book thus challenged the accepted view of both Victorian politics and Victorian sexuality. However, Walkowitz's focus at the end of the book is on the results of the campaign and the repeal of the Acts on the women's movement rather than the political structures and ideologies. The links between women's activities in their separate sphere and the public political world, whether in mid-nineteenth-century America or late nineteenth-century Britain were still open to further analysis.

One Hand Tied Behind Us arose directly from a precise location and a hunch on the part of two young women historians who were living in Lancashire and teaching in adult education. Jill Liddington and Jill Norris were aware of working-class women's involvement in radical politics and the trade union movement: their hunch was that such women would have played a significant part in the suffrage movement. The book is a narrative based on their examination of the plentiful evidence for this participation which they tracked down. They challenged the content of the history of suffrage, but they remained implicitly within a theoretical position which understood parliamentary politics to be highly significant, and associated independence with work outside the home. The core of their challenge to the dominant historical paradigm lay in their demonstration of working-class women's participation in the suffrage struggle. As Walkowitz had put it when she made a reference to *One Hand Tied Behind Us* in her introduction to the debate in *Feminist Studies*, 'women inhabited many female worlds in the nineteenth century, and their cultures were differentiated by class, race, and other social divisions'.[42] Despite the call for studies of relations between men and women, for a paradigm shift in methodology, the central focus of both these books was on the history of women precisely because there was, as the content of this study demonstrated, so much to be done. There was a continued recognition, as Sheila Rowbotham had put it, that 'we barely know what happened in the lives of the great mass of women'.[43]

British historians of women were, moreover, still struggling to have the validity of their enterprise fully recognised. A volume of essays on the writing of history was published in 1981 in Britain.[44] Significantly, only 10 per cent of the pages of *People's History and Socialist History* contained writings on women's history, and a quarter of those pages were included in a section on 'Sexual politics'. In his editorial preface to the volume Raphael Samuel, a well-respected and radical British labour historian, pointed out that historians 'are not given . . . to introspection about their work . . .', and that 'they instinctively reach for the "facts", and, rather than waste time in philosophical speculation, prefer to get on with the job'.[45] However, the book had its genesis in what Samuels referred to as 'the current debate on theory'.[46] His perception of the debate seemed to have been that it was the result of incursions from sociology, structuralism in particular. His reference to women's history ensued from an acknowledgement that 'our knowledge of the past is crucially shaped by the preoccupations we bring to bear on it, and that we can only interpret the evidence within the limits of an imaginative vision which is itself historically conditioned'. He did honour, albeit cursorily, the achievement of women's historians in questioning leading conceptual categories such as class, and in putting into question 'the whole mental landscape of socialist thought: sexuality and patriarchy cannot, in any simple way, be derived from property relationships; nor can modes of production – or notions of class consciousness – any longer be divorced from the crucial mediations of the home'. Sheila Rowbotham's assault on the concept of patriarchy, together with the response by Barbara Taylor and Sally Alexander, appeared in this volume. Other contributors on women's history included Anna Davin.[47] Davin focused on the contribution feminism was able to make to labour history, in particular the exposure of the sexual division of labour to historical analysis. Her understanding of feminist history, as opposed to women's history, was that it was not defined by subject matter, but rather by the questions it asked. It is not altogether clear what these questions would be, but they seem to be concerned with gender differences, and the formations of attitudes towards gender, although she does not use that term. At the end of her article she called for 'Comradely criticism and exchange' between feminist and socialist historians: 'fragmentation and resistance to new ideas only help the other side'.

Davin did not specify who was on the other side, but it was clear that the side she was on was firmly placed within the *History Workshop Journal* of which both she and Raphael Samuels were at that time editors, and of which Sheila Rowbotham was an associate editor. Barbara Taylor and Sally Alexander were also editors. All these women taught in adult education, like Jill Liddington and Jill Norris. The material of *Eve and the New Jerusalem*, Taylor's book on the socialist feminist struggles of the early nineteenth century, was presented in adult education courses for many years before it appeared in print. In her review of the book for the *Guardian*, Sheila Rowbotham recalled one such class sitting shivering in the basement of Essex Road Women's Centre. Evidence of both the increasing confidence of feminists involved in *History Workshop*, and also their wariness of their brother socialists, is to be found in the decision of the journal to change its subtitle from 'a journal of socialist historians' to 'a journal of socialist and feminist historians' in 1982. Justifying the decision, the editorial pointed out that the journal had from the start 'made the promotion and publication of feminist history one of its central concerns', but that the editors now believed that a clearer statement 'of our collective enterprise was needed. It was, they wrote, 'increasingly apparent that feminist ideals and demands cannot simply be subsumed under the socialist label. Many socialists are not feminists'.[48] Moreover feminist history through the questions it posed, the methodologies it used, and the 'sophistication of analytical approaches adopted . . . has now clearly moved into the frontiers of progressive historical writing'. The editors hoped that the change in the journal's title would 'encourage feminist writers to view it as *their* platform, and that this will simultaneously act as a constant spur to the editors to ensure that the *Journal* deserves the name it has taken'. In order to do this, it would be necessary for contributors to 'become sensitive to the central significance of sexual divisions in shaping both past and present'. Further evidence of the growing acceptance, at least among publishers, of women's studies as an academic discipline in Britain is apparent in the publication of a volume of essays in 1981 which 'documented the extent to which we (WOMEN) have been taken into account in various disciplines, and therefore, the extent to which we have begun to alter the power configurations of the construction of knowledge and in society'.[49] Dale Spender was the editor and she described how her passionate engagement in the women's movement in the late sixties had led her to ask the question: 'Why were women of the present cut off from women of the past and how was this achieved?' The 'simple answer' she found was that 'patriarchy doesn't like it'.[50]

The chapter in *Men's Studies Modified*, which looked at the impact of feminism on history, was written by Jane Lewis, and it was a thorough and cogent contribution to a developing historiography. Lewis reflected on the early seeds of the modern growth in women's history, in particular the privileging of 'the powerless and inarticulate' by the new social history.[51] She was critical of the omission of women from some of the crucial debates among labour historians, and provided an incisive critique of the inadequacies of family history. She divided the 'new women's history' into two categories: one which added more information, and the other which 'attempts to re-examine history from a "woman-centred" point of view, and involves asking new questions of new topics'. She described the latter approach as 'both more exciting and more valuable' because it led to the 'clarification and reinterpretation of the ideas we had about women's position in the past'. But she acknowledged the methodological problems which had arisen, referring to the – exclusively American – women's historians who had reviewed the methods they employed: Linda Gordon, Gerda Lerner, Carroll Smith-Rosenberg and Nathalie Zemon Davis. Lewis emphasised her own commitment to combining 'an understanding of theoretical concepts (often drawn from other disciplines) with careful research'.[52] She identified the potential for a strong theoretical framework which would 'make the consideration of gender as automatic as consideration of class'.[53]

Lewis's survey of the developments in women's history which follows is detailed, comprehensive and detached. She identified studies which had adopted a woman-centred point of view and as a result had altered historical perspectives on episodes in history such as the French Revolution, and the adoption of birth control methods, both of which drew attention to the tension between the awareness of women as agents, and as victims. She commended Carroll Smith-Rosenberg for 'finely drawn' studies of the relationships between doctor and patient, and Ellen Dubois for her 'satisfying challenge' to the rigidity of the public/private dichotomy.[54] Lewis understood patriarchy to be 'subject to changing definitions over time'; definitions not successfully integrated into feminist theory and analysis at the time she was writing.[55] Finally, Lewis gave her readers a glimpse of the complex process through which her own thinking went when considering the history of childbirth practices. Her intention was to demonstrate the painstaking steps which needed to be taken by an historian who wished to 'develop a woman-centred historical perspective and at the same time to add gender to the already established categories of analysis', while at the same time paying rigorous attention to the historical evidence.[56]

Lewis's emphasis on rigour may well be a reflection of the fact that she was in the forefront of the struggle to gain respect for women's history. She pointed out that in Britain, 'a feminist perspective is still regarded by many as biased history and graduate students must often fight to include the word feminist in their research titles'.[57] She was herself working in a sociology department and she identified the Sociology department at the University of Essex (which included Leonore Davidoff on its staff) as her one example of a place where 'the study of the sexual divisions in the past' was well established. Part of the problem, she recognised, was how few 'works of synthesis' existed to help women's historians to assess their own field of research. The task of writing such works was a daunting one, and the obstacles to such a venture would later be compounded by criticisms of the validity of writing what would be termed 'meta-narratives'. Lewis wrote one herself – *Women in England, 1870–1940: Sexual Divisions and Social Change*, published in 1984, which became a treasured text for students for at least a decade afterwards.[58]

Jane Lewis divided the structure of *Women in England* into a section on 'Family, marriage and motherhood' and one headed 'Employment'. In 'Women, lost and found' Lewis had been critical of the absence of a 'woman's point of view' from studies on the family, and had identified the significance of histories which 'stressed the relationship between family and work, between women's reproductive and productive life'.[59] She argued that women's values were deeply rooted in familial values and the decisions they made about work or politics were shaped by their strong links with the family. In an article which had been published in 1979, Rayna Rapp had criticised 'the acceptance of "the family" as a natural unit existing in separation from the total social formation'.[60] She argued that the family was a social construction whose 'boundaries are always decomposing and recomposing in continuous interaction with larger domains'. In a conclusion jointly composed with Ellen Ross and Renate Bridenthal, Rapp wrote that 'the family as an analytical category has only limited value for historical explanation'. Mary Ryan picked up this thread in her introduction to an analysis of writings on 'Domesticity' in America in the mid-nineteenth century which was published in 1982.[61] One purpose of the volume was 'to shed light on some of the conceptual and interpretative difficulties that inevitably accompany the accumulation of empirical evidence', and evidence on the complex history of the family had indeed been accumulating over the past decade. Data had been compiled on household size, membership, fertility, life-cycle changes, and sources of income. Another of Ryan's purposes was to scrutinise the 'gnarly conceptual problems that lurk in the relationship between women and the family'.[62] The weight of documentation supported the view that women's secondary status in society was associated with motherhood and domesticity, but Ryan did not want to 'build women's history around a search for feminist escape from the family' nor to 'pit women and the family in an adversary relationship'.[63] She saw the need to fill some of the gaps which she detected in the growing body of work on women, for example 'the vital connnection between male and female' and the 'historical specificity and variations in the institution of the family', by her collection of literary evidence.[64]

Ryan had identified as a problem for historians the presumption of 'an individualized female subject', and called for the 'individuality and subjectivity of women in history to be investigated rather than assumed'.[65] Historians of women were being drawn towards psychological interpretations of their material. In the last chapter, mention was made of the fact that Carroll Smith-Rosenberg had been tempted to 'elaborate a psychological interpretation' of nineteenth-century 'gynecological metaphors and formulations concerning puberty and menopause'.[66] Sally Aexander agreed with Ryan that 'if we are to pursue the history of women's experience and of feminism there can be no retreat from a closer enquiry into subjectivity and sexual identity'.[67] She made use of Jacques Lacan's 'psychoanalytical account of the unconscious and sexuality' in order to 'place subjectivity and sexual difference firmly at the centre of my research and historical writing'. Alexander had been an advocate of the appropriateness of the term patriarchy for the study of women's history, and later she would present patriarchy as a 'transitional term' which was 'rethought in the early 70s through the writing of Jacques Lacan'.[68] For Lacan, she wrote, the acquisition of subjectivity and sexual identity occurs simultaneously with language and is a continual, precarious and never completed 'process of differentiation, division and splitting . . .'.[69] The individual – especially the girl, given the way culture privileges masculinity – finds it difficult to align herself 'within the linguistic order, since there are as many different orders as there are discourses to structure them and always the possibility of more'. Antagonism and conflict are thus present in the very construction of the individual. Not only individual subjectivity, but all meaning arises from language alone: Sally Alexander added in parenthesis that this was a 'salutary, if familiar, reminder to the historian that historical reconstruction of the past is always through interpretation of the sources, which serve like memory-traces for the psychoanalyst, as the primary sources from which and over which we impose our own interpretations and causalities'. She stated that she did not intend to 'reconstruct the individual unconscious, or individual subjectivity (which may be glimpsed nevertheless by the historian through autobiography, memory or speech)'. What she intended was to 'emphasize that the symbolic sets the terms within which any social group must position itself and conceive of a new social order and that the symbolic has a life of its own'. She did not define the symbolic, but I think it can be assumed to be that which is represented, most often in language. Her second intention was to emphasise 'that human subjectivity shapes, as it is itself shaped by, political practice and language – it leaves its imprint there'. History offered 'the constant reshaping, reorganizing of the symbolization of difference, and the sexual division of labour', and the 'questions for the historian of feminism are why at some moments does sexual difference and division take on political significance – which elements in the organization are politicized, what are the terms of negotiation, and between whom?'.[70] Reading the rest of the paper in the light of the theoretical framework Alexander has set up makes one aware of her reliance on words rather than actions: it is very different from her study of 'Women's work in nineteenth century London' published eight years previously.

Alexander had left the unravelling of the polarities 'material/mental; true/false; cause/effect' to philosophers: other historians would later essay their own unravelling. The early eighties had seen women's history put down roots, begin to establish itself visibly in academia in the US. Research and writing by historians of women made extensive and meticulous use of traditional and new types of sources. Alongside this relatively conventional growth in the discipline the writings of Joan Kelly, Carroll Smith-Rosenberg and Sally Alexander presented fresh seeds of a challenge to the assumptions of traditional history. Jane Lewis had drawn together the work done by historians of women on either side of the Atlantic. In 1983 a volume of essays in the History Workshop series entitled *Sex and Class in Women's*

History was published which included contributions from both American and British historians of women.[71] The Editors were Judith Newton, Mary Ryan and Judith Walkowitz and their Introduction referred to the 'heritage of connection' between feminist writers across the Atlantic, identifying the points of agreement and disagreement. The British had placed an emphasis on class, while the Americans had developed 'a theory of gender and of women's culture'.[72] The 'heightened consciousness of gender' in the American experience had led to a rapid growth of women's studies within academia and publishing, a development 'which prompts British historians of women to marvel at the scale and institutional solidity of American scholarship about women'.[73] The editors looked to Joan Kelly's ' "doubled vision of feminist theory" ' to 'resolve the conflicts between radical-feminist and socialist-feminist, feminist and Marxist, American and British which results from attempts to reduce sex oppression to class interests on the one hand, and to see the relation of the sexes as always and ever the same, regardless of race, class or society, on the other'.[74] The volume included the essay on the family by Rayna Rupp, Ellen Ross and Renate Bridenthal mentioned above, and one on 'Class and gender in Victorian England' by Leonore Davidoff, who had been writing on Victorian women's history since the early 1970s and had contributed to the volume edited by Oakley and Mitchell described in Chapter Two. There were essays on black American women, and one on women's culture by Mary Ryan. The chapters of the book thus scrupulously covered the areas where debate among historians of women was taking place, but they did not make specific use of Kelly's construct of a 'doubled vision'. There still existed a space for the insertion of a theoretical framework which might draw together the variety of approaches adopted by historians of women: such a framework based on gender, a concept already in use, was put forward vigorously from the early eighties by Joan Scott.

Notes and references

1. Sheila Rowbotham, *Dreams and Dilemmas* (London, 1983), pp. 178–9.

2. Gerda Lerner, 'The majority finds its past', *Current History*, 70:416 (May, 1976), pp. 194–6.

3. Nathalie Zemon Davis, ' "Women's history" in transition: the European case', *Feminist Studies*, 3:3/4 (Spring/Summer, 1976), pp. 83–103.

4. Joan Kelly, 'The social relations of the sexes: methodological implications of women's history', *Signs*, 1:4 (Summer, 1976), pp. 809–23.

5. Joan Kelly, 'Did women have a Renaissance?', in Renate Bridenthal and Claudia Koonz, eds., *Becoming Visible: Women in European History* (Boston, Mass., 1977).

6. Sally Alexander, 'Women's work in nineteenth-century London; a study of the years 1820–1850', in A. Oakley and J. Mitchell, eds., *The Rights and Wrongs of Women* (London, 1976), p. 111.

7. Sheila Rowbotham, 'The trouble with patriarchy', *New Statesman* (December, 1979), reprinted in Raphael Samuel, ed., *People's History and Socialist History* (London, 1989), pp. 364–9.

8. Sally Alexander and Barbara Taylor, 'In defence of "patriarchy"', in ibid., pp. 370–3.

9. Michelle Rosaldo, 'The use and abuse of Anthropology', *Signs*, 5 (Spring, 1980), pp. 400–14.

10. Joan Kelly, 'The doubled vision of feminist theory', *Feminist Studies*, 5 (Spring, 1979), pp. 216–27.

11. Gerda Lerner, *The Creation of Patriarchy* (Oxford, 1986), p. 6.

12. Ibid., p. 7.

13. Gerda Lerner, 'Placing women in history: definitions and challenges', *Feminist Studies*, 3:1–2 (1978), pp. 5–14.

14. Gerda Lerner, *The Majority Finds Its Past* (Oxford, 1979), p. 180.

15. Ibid., p. 169.

16. Lerner (1979), p. vii.

17. Ibid.

18. Zemon Davis (1976), p. 93.

19. Carroll Smith-Rosenberg, *Disorderly Conduct: Visions of Gender in Victorian America* (Oxford, 1985), p. 30.

20. Nancy Cott, *The Bonds of Womanhood* (New Haven, Conn., 1977).

21. Ibid., p. 6.

22. Ibid., p. 7.

23. Ibid., p. 8.

24. Ibid., p. 5.

25. Ibid., p. 2.

26. Ibid., p. 197.

27. Ibid., p. 199.

28. Ibid., p. 194.

29. Ibid., p. 199.

30. Ibid., pp. 203–4.

31. Judith Walkowitz, 'Introduction to politics and culture in women's history', *Feminist Studies*, 6:1 (Spring, 1980), pp. 26–7.

32. Barbara Sicherman, 'American history', *Signs*, 1:2 (1975), pp. 476–7.

33. Ellen Dubois, 'Politics and culture in women's history', *Feminist Studies*, 6:1 (Spring, 1980), pp. 28–35.

34. Ellen Dubois, *Feminism and Suffrage: The Emergence of an Independent Women's Movement in America 1848–1869* (Ithaca, NY, 1978), p. 18.

35. Carroll Smith-Rosenberg, 'Politics and culture in women's history', *Feminist Studies*, 6:1 (Spring, 1980), pp. 55–63.

36. Buhle, ibid., pp. 37–41.

37. Lerner, ibid., pp. 49–54.

38. Kaplan, ibid., pp. 43–7.

39. Christine Stansell, 'Review essay', *Feminist Studies*, 6:1 (Spring, 1980), pp. 65–75.

40. Judith Walkowitz, *Prostitution and Victorian Society* (Cambridge, 1978). Jill Liddington and Jill Norris, *One Hand Tied Behind Us: The Rise of the Women's Suffrage Movement* (London, 1978).

41. Walkowitz (1978), p. 4.

42. Walkowitz (1980), p. 27.

43. Sheila Rowbotham, *Dreams and Dilemmas* (London, 1983), p. 179.

44. Samuel (1989).

45. Ibid., p. xl.

46. Ibid., p. lii.

47. Ibid., pp. 179–81.

48. '"History Workshop Journal" and feminism', *History Workshop Journal*, 13 (Spring, 1982), pp. 1–2.

49. Dale Spender, ed., *Men's Studies Modified: The Impact of Feminism on Academic Disciplines* (Oxford, 1981), p. 3.

50. Ibid., p. 13.

51. Ibid., p. 55.

52. Ibid., p. 57.

53. Ibid., p. 58.

54. Ibid., pp. 66, 68.

55. Ibid., p. 68.

56. Ibid., p. 64.

57. Ibid., p. 69.

58. Jane Lewis, *Women in England, 1870–1950: Sexual Divisions and Social Change* (Brighton and Bloomington, Indiana, 1984).

59. Spender, ed. (1981), p. 67.

60. Rayna Rapp, Ellen Ross and Renate Bridenthal, 'Examining family history', *Feminist Studies*, 5:1 (Spring, 1979), pp. 174–96.

61. Mary Ryan, *The Empire of the Mother: American Writing about Domesticity, 1830–1860* (New York, 1982).

62. Ibid., p. 4.

63. Ibid., p. 6.

64. Ibid., p. 10.

65. Ibid., pp. 6–7.

66. Smith-Rosenberg (1985), p. 196.

67. Sally Alexander, 'Women, class and sexual differences in the 1830s and 1840s: some reflections on the writing of a feminist history', *History Workshop Journal*, 17 (Spring, 1984), pp. 125–49.

68. Sally Alexander, *Becoming a Woman and Other Essays on 19th and 20th Century Feminist History* (London, 1994), p. xviii.

69. Alexander (1984), p. 133.

70. Ibid., pp. 134–5.

71. Judith Newton, Mary Ryan and Judith Walkowitz, eds., *Sex and Class in Women's History* (London, 1983).

72. Ibid., p. 3.

73. Ibid., p. 4.

74. Ibid., p. 5.

CHAPTER FOUR

Gender, a useful category of historical analysis 1983–7

In an article published in 1983 Joan Scott called for the 'articulation of gender (or sexual difference) as a category of historical analysis'.[1] Gender, Scott argued, was 'a conceptual perspective that makes possible a genuine "rewriting of history"'. Consideration in this chapter of the developments in women's history in the mid-eighties will be threaded through with references to Scott's clarion call. Debates over the relevance of class, over the validity and usefulness of the abstraction 'patriarchy', and about the relationship of women's culture to politics continued. Discussions about the relationship between contemporary feminism and the writing of the history of women also persisted, with male historians joining the debates. Although historians of women in Europe still felt that their work was embattled and remained on the margins, American historians were increasingly prolific and confident. The second half of the eighties saw the publication of important works by American and British historians of women: there was no uniformity in the way gender was methodologically employed but the use of gender as a category of analysis was invariably present in the approaches adopted.

Scott's 1983 article began with a survey of approaches to women's history by her contemporaries. Scott fully acknowledged the 'extraordinary diversity in topic, method and interpretation' in writings by historians of women, and she was determined to avoid the 'reductionism' involved in trying to track down in all the work done within 'a single interpretive or theoretical stance', and to root her critical evaluation of it in an acknowledgement of 'its complexity and confusions . . .'. She asserted that these confusions arose from the fact that studies of women's history were written in isolation from one another and they lacked 'a definable historiographic tradition within which interpretations are debated and revised'. Her article,

61

like Jane Lewis's contribution to *Men's Studies Modified*, gave a detailed survey of the developments in women's history of the nineteenth and twentieth century during the previous decade, but, unlike Lewis, she focused mainly on North American scholarship because of the volume of work undertaken there and because she found there 'the fullest elaboration of theoretical debates'. Scott's areas of scrutiny are also similar to those identified by Lewis: women's work; reproduction, including sexuality, the family, birth control, and the rise of medical science; the political involvement of women, including suffrage and the French Revolution. She surmised that most scholars working in the field assumed 'their work will transform history as it has been written and understood' but differed as to what needed to be done in order to achieve this end. Some retrieved information on women which was previously unavailable; others challenged received opinion about the nature and direction of change, while a smaller number used evidence about women to re-examine the organisation of societies and the dynamics of power. Unlike Jane Lewis, Scott does not give an example of how she would approach a particular research topic, and her references to the work of Taylor, Davidoff and Walkowitz suggest that she welcomed a variety of approaches, but saw the study of the relations between men and women as essential. She did not belittle the achievements of studies such as that of Liddington and Norris, which she describes as in 'the best traditions of the social histories of labour (that were inspired by the work of E.P. Thompson)', since they gave historical value to an experience which had been ignored. Scott placed this approach with its insistence on female agency alongside the work of Carroll Smith-Rosenberg and Nancy Cott. She hinted at a danger in this approach of failing to distinguish between 'the valuation of women's experience (considering it worthy of study) and the positive assessment of everything women said or did'. What it did do was to substitute women for men in history: what it did not do was the 'rewrite conventional history'. What Scott defined as the second approach was one which she associated with social history. The results of the support which social history had provided for women's history were the amassing of more information about, and the offering of explanations for the shape of women's working lives. But the challenge to 'rewrite history' had been stymied because 'most of the social history of women's work has been contained within the terms of social theories based on analytic categories that are mainly economic'. She also referred briefly to the use of the 'notion patriarchy' which she found was either ahistorical or again based directly on 'economic causes'.

Scott clearly valued the complexity of the history of women, but she seemed to want to suggest the possibility of some coherence within it. Her concern was that studies focused on women had not 'fundamentally altered' historians' understanding of 'social processes or social movements'. She believed this was because 'the issue of gender . . . has not been sufficiently singled out as either providing qualitatively different insights or as raising different kinds of analytic questions'. Scott's favoured approach was one she detected in the goals set out for women's history seven years earlier by Joan Kelly and Nathalie Zemon Davis. It was 'a method or procedure for investigation' rather than a single theory. She referred approvingly to Walkowitz's study of Victorian prostitution, identifying in particular Walkowitz's use of Foucault's 'suggestions' as her starting point. She also commended Leonore Davidoff's exploration of 'the ways in which individuals played with culturally defined categories of gender and class in her article on Arthur J. Munby', and Barbara Taylor's re-interpretation of Utopian Socialism for its consideration of 'the discourses and experiences of men and women' in parallel. Scott implicitly agreed with Ellen Dubois in her insistence that to ignore politics in 'the recovery of the female subject is to accept the reality of public/private distinctions and the separate or distinctive qualities of women's character and experience'. She advocated a 'realization of the radical potential of women's history' through 'the writing of narratives that focus on women's experience *and* analyse the ways in which politics constructs gender and gender constructs politics'. This formulation of the task of the historian of women was one that Scott asserted would begin 'the rewriting of history' by the 'exposure of the often silent and hidden operations of gender which are nonetheless present and defining forces of politics and political life'.

Scott's call for the use of gender as a 'useful category of historical analysis' was explained and developed more fully in 1986 in an article in the *American Historical Review*.[2] She identified 'gender' firstly as the term employed by American feminists to denote a rejection of biological determinism; as a relational term to stress the interconnectedness of the history of men and women, and thirdly as a concept used by those such as Joan Kelly to force a re-examination of the orthodox versions of history. But the tendency, she argued, was for gender to be used descriptively and for its use simply to mean that women were added on. Historians who were aware of this problem did search for theories that might 'explain the concept of gender and account for change'; one of those was 'patriarchy'. The problems she now found with theories of patriarchy were that they did not connect gender with other inequalities and they rested on ideas of physical difference. Scott went on to look at how Marxism was adopted by both American and British feminists, and argued that it offered no independent analytic status for gender. Psychoanalysis, she acknowledged, did avoid this problem but was exclusively fixed on the individual subject, and was inclined to universalise the categories and relationships of male and female, whereas she sought to encourage historians to historicise and deconstruct the terms of sexual difference. She looked specifically at Sally Alexander's use of Lacan, expressing an uneasiness about what she saw as the timeless quality of her formulation. She was also troubled by the binary opposition taken from Lacan and used by Alexander in writing that 'antagonism between the sexes is an unavoidable aspect of the acquisition of sexual identity'. She wanted instead to 'employ Jacques Derrida's definition of deconstruction' which would involve 'analyzing in context the way any binary opposition operates, reversing and displacing its hierarchical construction, rather than accepting it as real or self-evident or in the nature of things'. Such a process would be an essential component of the use of gender as an analytic category. This did not mean that historians would 'quit the archives', but that they would need to shift their focus from causes and explanations to meanings and processes. The concept of power as unified and coherent would need to be replaced by Foucault's idea of 'power as dispersed con-stellations of unequal relationships'. There would still be room for 'human agency as the attempt (at least partly rational) to construct an identity, a life, a set or relationships, a society within certain limits and with language . . .'. Towards the end of the essay Scott provided a full definition of her under-standing of gender, the core of which 'rests on an integral connection between two propositions: gender is a constitutive element of social relation-ships based on perceived differences between the sexes, and gender is a primary way of signifying relationships of power'. She advocated that his-torians 'treat the opposition between male and female as problematic rather than known, as something contextually defined, repeatedly constructed, then we must constantly ask not only what is at stake in proclamations or debates that invoke gender to explain or justify their positions but also how implicit understandings of gender are being invoked and reinscribed'. The examples she gave were drawn from political history, partly because 'the territory is virtually uncharted'.

This essay by Joan Scott would provide a methodological reference point for debates about the practice of historians of women for at least a decade. It was perhaps the burgeoning state of the practice of women's history which led her to attempt to provide a central focus for the work. Scott's article in *Past & Present* was part of a series on the current state of women's history, a series which in itself indicated the increasing respectability of the subject. In her notes Scott listed three American journals which published articles on women's studies, and one series of monographs, *Women and History*. British feminist historians published in *Feminist Studies* and the *History Workshop Journal*. The late seventies and early eighties saw the flowering of a feminist publishing venture launched in 1975 in Britain which was to provide a spectacular impetus to women's history. Its main contribution in its early years was probably its re-publication of historical sources such as *The Hard*

Way Up: The Autobiography of Hannah Mitchell (1977), *Maternity: Letters from Working Women* (1978), and *Roundabout a Pound a Week* (1979). Virago brought out Barbara Taylor's *Eve and the New Jerusalem* in 1983, and in the following year published for the first time *The Diaries of Hannah Cullwick, Victorian Maidservant*. The editor of these diaries was Liz Stanley, a lecturer in sociology, who had discovered the existence of the diaries when doing research on Arthur Munby and was astonished to find that they had never been published. A decade later she described how her own interpretation of Hannah Cullwick was at first overshadowed by that of those whom she saw as experts. Stanley described the complex process of change which took place in her readings of Hannah Cullwick, demonstrating to her own readers her commitment to the idea of historical knowledge as a process, not a product.[3] The vigour of women's history at the grass roots was apparent from the publication by Pandora, the paperback arm of Routledge and Kegan Paul, of *Discovering Women's History*, described on its back cover as 'a practical handbook for people who are prepared to venture into attics, art galleries, cinemas, libraries, museums and record offices in pursuit of the history of British women'.

The growing respectability of women's history as a discipline was evinced by the subject of an International Meeting of Experts on 'Theoretical frameworks and methodological approaches to studies on the role of women in history as actors in economic, social, political and ideological processes' convened by Unesco in Paris in November 1984. Some of the papers presented there, together with others commissioned by Unesco 'to round out the international coverage' were published in a book edited by S. Jay Kleinberg which appeared in 1988.[4] The scope of *Retrieving Women's History* demonstrated the desire to retrieve women from a historical silence in Asia, South America, the Indian subcontinent and Africa, as well as Europe and the USA. The stance of the authors was conservative in the sense that most of them did not offer any new methodical approaches, and the focus was, as the title suggested, mainly on retrieval: Kleinberg's introduction asserted that such a retrieval could 'lead us to change our basic understanding of what history itself is'.[5] She provided in that introduction a useful general summary of the areas of investigation and achievements of historians of women, together with an indication of the increase in the sources which they had used. She identified two vital questions which in her observation were raised by such work: 'To what extent is the history of women the same as feminist history? To what extent does writing about women's past imply an ideological unity or a common set of references among those who undertake it?' The second question does hint at a challenge to the traditional framework within which historians worked: 'To what extent does writing women back into history lead us to re-examine the institutions and events which have been the traditional objects of historical inquiry?'[6] Kleinberg's final assessment of the impact of the work of women's historians was traditional in the way it was couched: 'History will be a more accurate reflection of human experience for our endeavours.'[7]

The essay which provided the strongest theoretical component was by Joan Scott. Scott emphasised the theme of the volume in the title of her contribution: 'The Problem of Invisibility'. She, like other contributors, provided a history of the development of women's history in the geographical area she covered, the USA, and noted that the field had been able to 'establish a secure foothold in the academy'.[8] But Scott was, as always, concerned about the question of methodology, and she developed the same argument which she had presented in *Past & Present* and *American Historical Review*. She repeated her assertion that much of the work done on women had remained within the interpretive framework already in place. The work had thus served 'a compensatory purpose', and had advanced interpretation, but had not addressed directly 'certain more fundamental theoretical and methodological problems'.[9] These problems were raised when historians began to ask how and why women were invisible, and the result, Scott wrote, was 'an important discussion about the usefulness of gender as a category of analysis'.[10] She then again reviewed the theoretical approaches based on Marxism, the psychoanalytical writings of Lacan and the work of Foucault. She applauded this diversity of approach, seeing it as a 'healthy eclecticism', but declared: 'historians of women have begun to articulate the need for a method and theory that is definably feminist'.[11] Her contribution ends with the assertion that historians of women were confronted by questions about 'How and why ideas change; how ideologies are imposed, and how such ideas set the limits of behaviour and define the meaning of experience.' It was in the context of a perception of history as the history of ideas, then, that she returned to her understanding that what historians of women add to the 'discussion' of history 'is a preoccupation with gender; how the terms of sexual difference are defined discursively; how they differ for women and men; how they are changed or imposed; how, finally, they are reproduced'.[12]

The contribution on British women's history in this volume was by Anna Davin. She began by reviewing past generations of historians of women; examined the contributions made by labour history and social history to women's history, and reviewed the beneficial effects of the – albeit irksome – marginality of the discipline in the UK. She was very aware of the pressures on historians of women to find the time to teach, write, research, encourage other women, attend conferences (and, in her case, to contribute to volumes of essays on the state of the art!). Davin, like Scott, saw the need for historians of women to move beyond 'the initial question, "where were the women and what they were doing?"', and she referred to the social construction of femininity, to the question '"what is a woman?"' which historians were asking. But there is much less emphasis on ideas and language in Davin's essay, and much more on the economic and the material: she asserted the importance of getting 'the facts as accurate as possible'. Her concluding stance is a highly confident, ambitious and political one in which she perceived historians 'working towards a more complete understanding of the past', and also 'contributing to the transformation of society'.[13]

There is a secure confidence in the writing of Scott and Davin which is also apparent in the examples of work being done by historians contained in *Retrieving Women's History*. Jane Lewis contributed an essay which provided an exemplary analysis of the sexual division of work in late nineteenth century England as 'part of the wider gender order'.[14] She pointed out that historians had tended to 'treat work in the family and work in the labour market dichotomously', and that 'women's position in the family is invoked to explain their position in the labour market' because 'work is not thought of as part of the gender order. Rather, the sexual division of work is made to fit already existing frameworks of explanation'.[15] Her understanding was that women's work was 'doubly gendered, first being confined to "feminine" tasks, whether paid or unpaid, and second being subordinated to men's work both at home and in the workplace'.[16] The nature and conditions of women's work 'were not determined solely by autonomous changes in the structure of the economy, but rather should be considered as part of the construction of maculinity and femininity', which themselves were subject to change and could be analysed.[17] Lewis thus analysed changes in ideas without abandoning the task of investigating changes in the material world.

While increasing assurance is apparent among Anglo-Saxon historians, there was less confidence in the potency of women's history among continental European historians of women. The voice of French women historians was heard by English readers of *Retrieving Women's History* in a chapter by Michelle Perrot. She first reviewed the 'stage' reached in the 'History of Women' in France. Perrot understood the women's movement and the spate of questions that it entailed, as providing the impetus for a history of women. The tentativeness of the early forays were expressed in the title of the first courses offered at the University of Paris in 1973: 'Have women a history?'[18] Journals were launched at the end of the seventies, a few posts in universities established and research funding initiated. But history, a 'highly esteemed branch of knowledge' in France, was still largely a male preserve. Her assessment of her discipline was that it was 'fragile and reversible, and the permanent infrastructure on which it rests is alarmingly weak'.[19] The evolution of subject-matter which Perrot traced was similar to the Anglo-Saxon pattern: women were first studied as vicitims and then as agents. Focus on 'bodily issues: pregnancy, childbirth, prostitution' was followed by an emphasis on work. Writings on the borderline between literature and history had looked at representations of women, and the history of feminism was beginning to attract attention. Lastly, she identified the current perception of the history of women as 'the history of relations between the sexes'.[20] Turning her attention to sources, she stressed the importance of 'approaching traditional sources from a different angle'; making greater use of sources dealing with 'commonplace events and private life, which tended to be neglected because of their insignificance'; recognising what literary sources can offer a historian, and making careful use of invaluable oral records.[21] The current burning questions for Perrot were to do with power. She echoed the debates among American historians (although her reference is to Italian historians) about the nature of the power of women and the distinctiveness of women's 'culture'. Perrot's closing passages are more cautious than those of the Anglo-Saxon historians. She agrees with Davin's aim of attaining a 'better overall understanding' by 'placing the relations between the sexes at the centre of historical research', but she does not think that claiming an ' "epistemological break" ' as a result of feminist research is justified. Different questions were being asked, but she was uncertain about the capacity of women's history 'to change the status quo' or to 'make people see things from a different angle', and she asks whether it might be 'only a projection of our fantasies?'.[22]

Michelle Perrot had expressed her cautions to her fellow historians of women concerning the continued marginality of their discipline in a collection of essays she herself had edited and which was published in 1984.[23] Perrot described the essays included not as a report on progress which had been done elsewhere, but as attempts 'to measure the difficulties, both extrinsic and, above all, intrinsic'.[24] Reflecting back on the 'history of bodies' which had been the main focus at first of women's history, she asserted that 'women's history must, and in fact does, go beyond this'.[25] The change in direction would be accomplished by 'posing the question of the relationship between the sexes as central'.[26] In Anglo-Saxon terms this meant 'gender' for which there was no equivalent word in French. Arlette Farge, in an essay in the same volume, did in fact provide an assessment of what women's history had achieved. She concluded that as 'this field of research is at last recognized and accepted', the effect was that it was 'carried on by many people without there necessarily being political links between it and its authors'.[27] What she questioned was the continued fascination with 'normative' texts witnessing to the oppression of women; she advocated attention to 'normative texts on the subject of men'. Clearly uncomfortable with ideas of progress or of a 'permanent and unchanging' low status, Farge envisaged history 'full of contradictions, of alternating currents, of overlapping events where consistency and inconsistency both have their place'.[28] She finished with a strong invocation of the importance of 'a history of the tensions between masculine and feminine roles', a history which would make 'a meticulous record of the changes and differences 'in relations between "the sexes"'. These relations, she believed, varied over the centuries, and according to social class; they also fulfilled a number of functions at any one time. The historian's task was 'to discover these functions and the way in which they arose and come into conflict with one another'.[29] Scott's call for the use of gender was clearly being heard, or had already been conceived of, by historians of women in France.

The flowering of women's history in the mid-eighties is apparent in another collection of essays published in the mid-eighties. British and American historians of women again came together to contribute a reply to the question 'What is Women's History', posed by the popular journal *History Today* in its edition of June, 1985. Olwen Hufton, who had contributed to the articles in *Past & Present*, was the author of the opening essay.[30] She put forward in plain language what she saw as the 'triple commitment' which writing a history of women implied. The first was to 'discern women's past role and situation'; the second to give the history of the period 'a gender dimension' (which she paraphrased as suggesting areas and issues where women influenced the course of events), and to examine the assumptions about men and women which lay behind the sources used by historians: the history of *mentalités*. This last was a peculiarly French conception which had arisen from the group of historians involved in the journal *Annales*. There is no satisfactory English translation; the nearest single word might be 'ideologies', but without the Marxist undertones of this word. Hufton wanted ideas to be understood in the context of 'the practicalities of existence', using the findings of demographic research as 'an excellent *factual* framework'. Her own purpose in writing women's history was to 'generate some appreciation of the struggle' of women in the past; a 'survival process' which she saw as 'in the main weighted more heavily on women than men'.

One man was included among the contributors to this issue of *History Today*; James McMillan who had published on the women's movement in France.[31] The other authors included Nathalie Zemon Davis, Linda Gordon, Anna Davin and Jane Rendall, who was emerging as one of the most respected British historians of feminism.[32] All the contributors divided the discipline into different approaches, broadly along the lines of the need to recognise that women had a history of their own, to discern in gender a powerful determining factor, and to make a difference to historical interpretation. They all asserted the importance of the challenge which women's history presented to the understanding of political structures. Zemon Davis declared that what was happening to women's history was that 'it was being extended to men. Sexual identity is an historical construction for both sexes . . .'. Angela John reflected the continuing preoccupations of British historians of the nineteenth century in her emphasis on the need to 'question both the workings of patriarchy and the pervasiveness of class'. Linda Gordon pointed out that women's history was not new, that it 'existed in relation to an active or dormant women's rights struggle', and that it was 'being defined in practice'. Jane Rendall called for references to gender to be as automatic as references to class: 'That way, our history will be the history of humanity.' Anna Davin suggested an answer to Kleinberg's question about the difference between women's history and feminist history. She distinguished women's history – defined by its subject matter, women – from feminist history, 'defined by its conscious standpoint – feminism'. Her understanding of feminism was implicit in her statement that: 'Feminist historians start consciously with the experience and recognition of women's oppression in their own society, and the desire to end it . . .'. Given this understanding it is not surprising that she detected a tension between the historian and the feminist, but she described this tension as 'creative'.

The tension between feminism and the writing of history is apparent in some responses in the early eighties by male historians to the enterprise of women's history. In a Review Essay published in 1980 Richard Evans, who had published work on women in Germany, complained of a tendency among historians of women to put 'reclamation before understanding in her hierarchy of intentions'.[33] He suggested that 'the efforts of women's history to recover the past can replace ignorance with condescension; and condescension not just towards men, but towards women as well, for their failure to live up to the standards of women's historians in the present day.' He accepted the validity for the 'women's liberation movement of the present day' of heroines from the past, but he urged historians of women to move beyond 'the elementary task of recovery to a cross-fertilization of women's history with social, economic and political history . . .'. Three years later, James McMillan and Brian Harrison were stung into a response to a review article which had criticised their own work on women.[34] Patricia Hilden had linked the surge in women's history to the understanding of modern feminists that 'successful politics in the present must grow out of an historical analysis', and she wanted feminist historians to 'strike a balance between present politics and a commitment to history'.[35] She detected prejudices in McMillan's selection of material in his study of women in France in the period 1870 to 1944. She described Brian Harrison's book on anti-suffragism in Britain as 'a monument to unconscious sexism'. Hilden's ideal was a history which included 'men's and women's activities as an integral part of the narrative'.

In their reply to Hilden, Harrison and McMillan sought grounds on which 'feminists and historians can fruitfully co-operate'. Their article is informed by a strong sense of what the constituents are of 'good women's history', which were 'scholarly methods of documentation and rational argument'. They accepted that a feminist commitment lends 'impetus and insight to a historian of women', but they averred that 'women's history can no more be confined to feminists than labour history can be assigned exclusively to the socialist . . .'. They accused feminists of being unable to 'cope with anti-feminist attitudes in the past', and asserted the importance for the historian of 'portraying and analysing unfashionable ideas, with as much attempt at comprehension as he can muster . . .'. At the end of their article they offered a statement of their attitude to women's history whose essence was the importance of avoiding the segregation of women from 'the mainstream of historical writing'. Their overall aim sounded similar to that of Hilden: 'an expanded and invigorated total history which will take as full account of women's distinctive experience as of men's'.

Where Harrison and McMillan offered advice to historians of women, Lawrence Stone laid down 'ten commandments which should, in my opinion, govern the writing of women's history at any time and in any place'.[36] The first of these was: 'Thou shalt not write about women except in relation to men and children. Women is not a distinct caste, and their history is a story of complex interactions.' The third commandment was: 'Thou shalt not forget that in the past nearly all women paid at least lip service to the idea that they were in all respects inferior to men, as ordained by God.' Stone's confidence in his unchallengeable knowledge of the past is apparent in the seventh of his commandments: 'Thou shalt not exaggerate the importance in the past of gender over that of power, status, and wealth', and in the ninth: 'Thou shalt be clear about what constitutes real change in the experience and treatment of women.' This admonition is echoed in numbers four and eight which order historians 'not to confuse prescriptive norms with social reality', and not to use the biographies of a few women to describe the experience of the majority of women. The implicit assumption behind Stone's dictates is that historians of women were failing to live up to the basic requirements of scholarly study, and that there was a commonly accepted view of what these requirements are. The same assured standpoint emerged in a review by G.R. Elton of Joan Kelly's *Women, History and Theory*.[37] The essence of Elton's criticism of the book is that Kelly's suggested framework 'does not embody an acceptable way of treating historical evidence – and that remark springs from what I know about the past, not from a nonexistent prejudice against women'.[38] Elton also viewed feminist historians as threatening the 'disintegration' of 'the history of humanity' which, from his perspective 'has long since managed to attend to both kinds of human beings'.

One historian of women who acknowledged that she was motivated by feminist political 'aspirations' provided an argument to support the case that this did not invalidate her work. Linda Gordon described the tension between historian and feminist, which Anna Davin had described as creative, in a chapter in *Feminist Studies/Critical Studies*.[39] She first recognised the work of previous generations of women's historians whose influence had been negligible, partly as a warning to her own, increasingly confident generation of the fate which might overtake them. She repeated her belief expressed in her contribution to *History Today*, that the attempt to reconstruct history which she and her contemporaries were engaged in was no new task, but one that 'many groups battling for political power have done before'.[40] She saw the academic and political impulses of women's history being channelled in two directions; towards truth and myth respectively. She sought a method which lay between these paths, accepting the need 'to create myths to serve our aspirations', but refusing to abandon what she referred to as the historian's 'equivalent to the Hippocratic oath' enjoining the historian 'to present all, or a representative sample, of the evidence relevant to a given enquiry; to search hard for the same; to seek out bits of evidence that might defeat our argument'. This perspective was firmly rooted in a traditional understanding which was proving to be durable. Indeed, Gordon rejected the notion that there existed a unique feminist methodology. The 'liminal' method she advocated was 'a condition of being constantly pulled, usually off balance, sometimes teetering wildly, almost always tense . . . the very desire to find a way to relax the tension is a temptation that must be avoided'.[41] The questions which she used as case-studies of this method were the co-existence of domination and resistance; the boundaries between the social and the political which arose from restrictive definitions of power, and the emphasis on 'difference' which could and did sometimes 'function to obscure domination'.[42] The final section of the chapter focused on 'the political import' of her message. She distinguished between feminism, which she defined as 'a critique of male supremacy, formed and offered in the light of a will to change it', while accepting that there was great variety within it, and 'female thought, women's culture, and female consciousness'.[43] It was necessary, she concluded, for feminist scholarship which 'focused on liberation' to criticize and even reject, 'part of what constituted female'.[44]

Linda Gordon believed that knowledge of the history of the feminist tradition 'served as a corrective to dogmatism, if nothing else'.[45] In 1987 another American historian added to the increasingly sophisticated history of political feminism, one that was developing as contemporary feminism became more multiple and complex. Nancy Cott, the author of *Bonds of Womanhood*, brought out a second major study, this time of the early twentieth century, in a book entitled *The Grounding of Modern Feminism*.[46] Cott acknowledged 'astute and constructive commentary' from Linda Gordon, and the 'comradely enthusiasm and longstanding willingness to share her knowledge' of Ellen Dubois, Juliet Mitchell and Judith Butler. She stated in her opening sentence that the book was 'about the time when the word *feminism* came into use in the United States, and the women who used it'.[47] As she pointed out, historians had used the word feminism retrospectively and carelessly. The 1920s had been denoted as the time of the demise of feminism without a considered recognition that 'the name and the phenomenon had just recently cropped up'. Cott's argument in the book, as the title indicates, is that 'the new language of Feminism marked the end of the woman movement and embarkation on a modern agenda. Women's efforts in the 1910s and 1920s laid the groundwork and exposed the fault lines of modern feminism'.[48] The faultlines lay along the tension between individualism, its 'investment in individual self-expression', and the assertion of a common cause for women.[49] Cott's view was that the tension 'between emphasis on the rights that women (like men) deserved and emphasis on the particular duties or services that women (unlike men) could offer society' was not debilitating , but was a double-lensed view which women were able to sustain until the vote was obtained. Indeed, Cott argued, this tension 'needed to be embraced rather than avoided under the name *feminism*'. Women in the 1960s had reclaimed feminism 'as a term of unity, to transcend the divisions between women's liberation and women's rights' which had become so vividly apparent fifty years before, but in the late twentieth century Cott's observation was that 'not only women but also feminisms grow towards the plural'.[50] Her book was thus clearly informed by the context in which she was writing, and although there is no reference to the current debate about methodology, Cott's description of what she sought to do resonates with Joan's Scott's demands. It was 'principally a study of consciousness', one which examined 'feminist intentions', and the consequent 'resistance', including that arising from 'resignation to the established forms in which gender relations are enmeshed'. Her interest, she wrote, was 'less in bringing renown to the little-known names of the women herein than in exploring their outlooks in order to suggest what was possible and likely among a larger generality of women'.[51] The year before Cott's book was published, Sandra Stanley Holton examined the ideology of the British suffrage movement in the years 1900–18 and came to conclusions similar to those of Cott.[52] Holton argued that most suffragists 'appeared unconscious of the potential contradictions' between a case for women's emancipation based on women's difference from men, and 'a more deliberately rationalistic, humanistic conception of feminism' which viewed the vote as a human right.[53] She claimed that the suffragist conception of the power of the vote was one that aspired to 'reconstuct society in accordance with female values and needs'.[54] Holton went beyond the intended scope of Cott's study when she claimed that the significance of the suffrage movement was necessary for a proper understanding of Edwardian politics.

Holton is British and her study, unlike Cott's, does not appear to be influenced by the ideas which Joan Scott had drawn together in *Gender: A Useful Category of Historical Analysis*. Scott's influence as 'teacher, critic, mentor, colleague, friend' was openly acknowledged by another American historian, Susan Kingsley Kent, in *Sex and Suffrage in Britain, 1860–1914*.[55] Kent offered a study of the longer-term suffrage movement, and one that also had implications, she argued, for 'the entire women's movement of the second half of the nineteenth century'.[56] She came somewhere near Holton's perspective in arguing that 'feminists sought to eliminate separate spheres altogether and to bring the positive qualities associated with women to society as a whole'.[57] But her greater emphasis on sexuality and her focus on 'voices, language, and ideas'; her statement that she was not writing a social history lifts her study away from the organisations and events of the period, and puts a different slant on her interpretation of the meaning of the vote to suffragists: 'The vote became both the symbol of the free, sexually autonomous woman and the means by which the goals of feminist sexual culture were to be attained.' The demand for enfranchisement, in Kent's view, 'was a direct strike at the very seat and symbolic locus of patriarchal power'.[58]

Joan Scott's emphasis on language, her affirmation that 'deconstruction'of texts, as defined by Derrida, was a central task for the historian, linked the methodology of the historian with that of the literary critic. Carroll Smith-Rosenberg was also increasingly focusing on voices, language and ideas. In her opening essay in *Disorderly Conduct*, she set out her understanding of the way language could be used to provide an 'analytic model that would reflect the diversity and fluidity of social relations'.[59] In this essay, she was specific in her definition of language as including 'dress and food codes, religious rituals, theories of disease aetiology, the varied forms of sexuality'.[60] She described how she had begun 'to examine women's and men's images and metaphors, testing for similarities and differences, to explore the ways language changes across time, between cultures and classes, to seek out the complex ways words both reflect and alter the world in which they are spoken . . .'. Although she stated clearly that '[T]he complex of reality will always elude the conceptual systems we construct for its capture', she 'felt that the richness and diversity of language . . . underscores the diversity and ambiguity that characterize all human experience, men's as much as women's'.[61] Although she is starting perhaps from a different place, Smith-Rosenberg's description of what she was doing in her work as a historian in this 1985 essay comes close to Joan's Scott's objective: 'By tracing differences between nineteenth-century women's and men's mythic constructs, I sought to re-create the way gender channelled the impact of social change and the experience and exercise of power.'[62]

Carroll Smith-Rosenberg also contributed the second essay on history to the interdisciplinary collection in *Feminist Studies/Critical Studies*. 'Writing history: language, class, gender' begins with the statement that historians were becoming increasingly sensitive to the power of words as a result of 'an active interchange between historians and literary theorists', such as M.M. Bakhtin and Hayden White.[63] Smith-Rosenberg quoted with some anxiety the argument of Nancy Partner, a medieval historian, that '"the whole of historical discourse is calculated to induce a sense of referential reality in a conceptual field with no external reference at all"', so that history had become '"the definitive human audacity imposed on formless time and meaningless event with the human meaning-maker language"'. She did not grapple with this perspective directly, although she noted the irony if feminist historians were to relinquish their grasp on the world just as 'feminist literary critics have begun to look beyond the words to study historical worlds'. She also noted that acceptance of the historical nihilism presented by Hayden White and Partner would involve the loss for the feminist historian of 'that aspect of the world we are most committed to knowing: women'. She then got to grips with the challenge of these ideas for historians of women, suggesting that 'rather than seeking to transcend the complexity of our semantic existence, let us meticulously trace it by analyzing the process by which words are formed out of experiences and experiences are shaped by words'.[64] She made use of Foucault's understanding of words as 'the point of intersection between the world of tangible "things" and the minds that respond to those "things"'; in her own construction, 'imaginative mediations of social experiences'. If language reflects experience, she argued, then in any society a multiplicity of languages would co-exist, 'reflecting the diversity of experiences across and within gender and class'. She acknowledged a debt to Bakhtin's theory of the dialectic between the dominant '"unitary"' language and the linguistic diversity in the form of dialects which challenges it. She proceeded to make use of these concepts to analyse one particular example of 'a female social dialect', that of the New York Female Moral Reform Society, as 'a first step toward an appreciation of the complexity of "language" and toward an understanding of the complex interaction of class and gender . . .'.[65] Her analysis led her to conclude that the Society had constructed 'a sexual and social vocabulary that offered a clear alternative within the dominant bourgeois discourse'.[66]

Joan Scott and Carroll Smith-Rosenberg's thinking was influenced by what were coming to be known as postmodernist or poststructuralist theories of knowledge. The impact of these ideas was apparent in a somewhat heterogeneous collection of essays published in 1987 under the title *Behind the Lines*.[67] At the end of the introduction the editors wrote that the essays: 'provide readings of a variety of wartime discourses ranging from the semiotics of the division of labor in defense industries to women's poetry and fiction, from the dominant to the oppositional. These readings are, by definition, resisting – that is, they refuse to accept the tacit categories the discourses enfold and attempt to enforce, but rather seek to expose systems of gender and analyze their inner workings'.[68] The understanding of historical knowledge contained within this passage is not shared by all the contributors, but it demonstrates the influence of the ideas of poststructuralism on historical studies and the inter-disciplinary roots of such influence. As with many collections of essays, the starting point for this one had been a conference, in this case a 'Workshop on Women and War' held at Harvard in 1984. The intention had clearly been to bring together academics from a variety of disciplines. Of the four editors, one was an American historian, one a Professor of Humanities and Modern Languages in England, one a Professor of English and one a Professor of Political Science in Canada. Of the other sixteen authors, three were Professors of English (all American), six were historians, six were social scientists, including a psychologist with a PhD in Comparative Literature, and one a doctoral candidate in a department of French studies. The opening essay was by Joan Scott. Interestingly, her approach is much less imbued with poststructuralist perspectives and language than the introduction. Her theme was once again the need to use gender as a category of analysis for the rewriting of history. She expressed surprise at the 'resistance of so many historians . . . to changes in their own discipline', but saw the benefits of this resistance in that it revealed the 'connections between professional politics and intellectual inquiry', and provided a stimulus to an examination of different approaches to the study of history.[69] She also recognised that the writing of women's history has been neither uniform nor coherent, and that the essays in *Behind the Lines* adopted diverse ways of investigating women in the specific context of two world wars. But these essays go some way to answering the question which Scott wanted to ask; not the conventional question of the impact of war on women, but what the history of women reveals about the politics of war.[70]

Scott declared at the start of her essay: 'History has become an increasingly complicated project over the course of the last two decades . . . The profusion of histories has created a sense of fragmentation and confusion.'[71] Not all her contemporaries would have agreed with this in a period which produced books such as *Family Fortunes: Men and Women of the English Middle Class* by Leonore Davidoff and Catherine Hall.[72] This book combined a tradition of thorough scholarship with a recognition of the significance of women's experience in history. The authors used gender as a category of analysis to challenge perceptions of the motors of social change in a particular period, although not precisely in the way recommended by Scott. *Family Fortunes* seemed to be the book that historians of women in Britain had been waiting for, and it became a canonical text for British women's historians in particular until the early nineties. Both authors had been writing on class and gender in the Victorian period since the late seventies. Davidoff is an American who had studied the employment of married women in England in the 1950s as 'a nascent sociologist'.[73] She then 'left the public world of work for a dozen years of housewifery, childrearing and helping to care for an elderly relative'.[74] When she returned to social and historical research, the questions which her experience during those years had raised about the division of labour and the radical differences between the world of work and the world of home resurfaced. From 1974 onwards she published essays and articles on domestic activities, and on the relationships rooted in the home. Davidoff was teaching at Essex when Catherine Hall went there to an MA in 1975: at the time it was the only university in the country where it was possible to study women's history as part of a postgraduate course. Their work together began in 1978 as a joint research project. Catherine Hall had become part of the women's movement in a moment of intense recognition when she was the mother of a young child and a university wife, trying to do research into medieval history under the inspiration of Rodney Hilton.[75] She abandoned this lonely task for involvement in the women's movement but did not abandon history. She, like other British historians of women, found adult education to be a 'facilitating framework for the development of new kinds of course and new areas of study'.[76] She helped initiate courses which put women back into history at Birmingham University's Extra-Mural Department, and was part of a feminist research group which was set up. After an encounter with feminist history written by American feminists, she wrote 'The history of the housewife'. The first version of this was published in 1973 and Hall herself reckons it 'has the hallmarks of this early attempt to link the new language of feminism with a reworked Marxism'.[77]

The 'Acknowledgements' page in *Family Fortunes* opens with the statement: 'The origins of this study lie in the Women's Liberation Movement and the questions which feminist history has raised over the past fifteen years. We continue to be deeply indebted to the existence of the feminist movement.'[78] They acknowledged the help and support of Sally Alexander, Anna Davin, Barbara Taylor, and – bearing witness to the links with women's historians across the Atlantic – Martha Vicinus and Judith Walkowitz. The subject matter of the book was 'the ideologies, institutions and practices of the English middle class from the end of the eighteenth to the mid-nineteenth centuries.'[79] The authors stated aim was to insert an awareness of the con-stitutive role of gender into an historical analysis, and, after picking their way through the 'use of gender terms as stand-ins for socially valued or derogated attributes', and the presentation of institutions and organisations which were gendered as neutral, their conclusion was that the ideology of domesticity and the concept of separate gender spheres gave a distinctive form to an emerging middle-class identity.[80]

Family Fortunes is a solid historical text, based on meticulous research, using evidence from sources such as censuses, wills, parish records, memoirs and contemporary writings from diaries to sermons. It assumes that direct conclusions can be drawn about people's lives from what they wrote about them. Two years later another book was published which was also to be influential among historians of women, but which used a different language and was based on different assumptions about how it might be possible to understand the 'ideological work of gender'. Mary Poovey's approach in *Uneven Developments*, which will be described in the next chapter, was strongly shaped by the challenge to the nature of historical knowledge truth contained in the ideas of Foucault and other 'deconstructive literary critics'.[81]

In the mid-eighties, gender was, as Scott had recommended, widely and effectively used as a category of analysis, but it was used in different ways. Scott herself drew on the ideas of Derrida to develop an understanding of the use of gender as a category for analysis through the deconstruction of texts in order to understand how difference, in particular sexual difference, was used to establish meaning and to legitimise power. She believed that this understanding of gender would transform the practice of historians in a way that feminist approaches had not so far been able to. While this perspective was not widely shared there was agreement that there was still work to be done on ensuring that women's contributions were recounted, and that the consequences of such history writing would be to change understandings on a wider scale. While the meanings of feminism in the past, and the links between feminism and the writing of history, were explored by women historians, some male historians had expressed their uneasiness about the feminist input into the writing of history. Such a reaction was indicative of way historians of women in Europe, while often operating still on the margins, was challenging the centre. In the US the discipline was growing fast and becoming increasingly influential.

Notes and references

1. Joan Wallach Scott, 'Women in history: the modern period', *Past and Present*, 101 (1983), pp. 141–57.

2. Joan Wallach Scott, 'Gender: a useful category of historical analysis', *American Historical Review*, 91:5 (1986), pp. 1053–75.

3. Liz Stanley, *The Auto/Biographical I: The Theory and Practice of Feminist Auto/Biography* (Manchester, 1992), pp. 158–80.

4. S.J. Kleinberg, ed., *Retrieving Women's History: Changing Perceptions of the Role of Women in Politics and Society* (Oxford and New York, 1988).

5. Ibid., p. ix.

6. Ibid., p. x.

7. Ibid., p. xii.

8. Ibid., p. 9.

9. Ibid., pp. 12–13.

10. Ibid., p. 13.

11. Ibid., p. 16.

12. Ibid., p. 29.

13. Ibid., p. 78.

14. Ibid., p. 151.

15. Ibid., p. 150.

16. Ibid., p. 163.

17. Ibid., p. 164.

18. Ibid., p. 43.

19. Ibid., p. 45.

20. Ibid., p. 46.

21. Ibid., pp. 47–9.

22. Ibid., pp. 56–7.

23. Michelle Perrot, ed., *Writing Women's History* (Oxford, 1984).

24. Ibid., p. 4.

25. Ibid., pp. 6–7.

26. Ibid., p. 8.

27. Ibid., p. 19.

28. Ibid., p. 21.

29. Ibid., p. 23.

30. Olwen Hufton, 'What is women's history?', *History Today* (June 1985), pp. 38–40.

31. Ibid., p. 40.

32. Ibid., pp. 40–8.

33. Richard J. Evans, 'Women's history: the limits of reclamation', *Social History*, v:2 (May 1980), pp. 273–81.

34. Brian Harrison and James McMillan, 'Some feminist betrayals of women's history', *Historical Journal*, 26:2 (1983), pp. 375–89.

35. Patricia Hilden, 'Women's history: the second wave', *Historical Journal*, 25:2 (1982), pp. 501–12.

36. Lawrence Stone, 'Only women', *New York Review of Books*, 32:6 (11 April 1985), pp. 21–2.

37. G.R. Elton, *American Scholar*, 54:3 (Autumn 1985).

38. G.R. Elton, 'The reader replies', *American Scholar*, 55:2 (Spring, 1986), pp. 286–7.

39. Teresa de Lauretis, ed., *Feminist Studies/Critical Studies* (Indiana, 1986).

40. Ibid., p. 20.

41. Ibid., p. 22.

42. Ibid., p. 26.

43. Ibid., pp. 29–30.

44. Ibid., p. 30.

45. Ibid., p. 30.

46. Nancy F. Cott, *The Grounding of Modern Feminism* (New Haven, Conn., 1987).

47. Ibid., p. 3.

48. Ibid., p. 4.

49. Ibid., p. 282.

50. Ibid., pp. 20, 283.

51. Ibid., p. 9.

52. Sandra Stanley Holton, *Feminism and Democracy* (Cambridge, 1986).

53. Ibid., p. 28.

54. Ibid., p. 18.

55. Susan Kingsley Kent, *Sex and Suffrage in Britain, 1860–1914* (Princeton, New Jersey, 1987).

56. Ibid., p. 16.

57. Ibid., p. 183.

58. Ibid., pp. 23, 13.

59. Carroll Smith-Rosenberg, *Disorderly Conduct* (Oxford, 1985), p. 42.

60. Ibid., p. 43.

61. Ibid., p. 42.

62. Ibid., p. 45.

63. De Lauretis (1986), p. 31

64. Ibid., p. 32.

65. Ibid., p. 38.

66. Smith-Rosenberg is using discourse in the sense defined in the work of Michel Foucault. Joan Wallach Scott in 'Deconstructing equality-versus-difference; or, the uses of post-structuralist theory for feminism', *Feminist Studies*, 4:1 (Spring, 1988), pp. 33-50, defined discourse as 'a historically specific structure of statements, terms, categories and beliefs'.

67. Margaret Randolph Higonnet, Jane Jenson, Sonya Michel and Margaret Collins Weitz, eds., *Behind the Lines: Gender and the Two World Wars* (New Haven, Conn., 1987).

68. Ibid., p. 17.

69. Ibid., p. 21.

70. Ibid., p. 30.

71. Ibid., p. 21.

72. Leonore Davidoff and Catherine Hall, *Family Fortunes: Men and Women of the English Middle Class 1780-1850* (London, 1987).

73. Leonore Davidoff, *Worlds Between: Historical Perspectives on Gender and Class* (Cambridge, 1995), p. 2.

74. Ibid., p. 3.

75. Anna Coote and Beatrix Campbell, *Sweet Freedom: The Struggle for Women's Liberation* (London, 1982), pp. 15, 25.

76. Catherine Hall, *White, Male and Middle-Class: Explorations in Feminism and History* (Cambridge, 1992), p. 7.

77. Ibid., p. 6.

78. Davidoff and Hall (1986), p. 11.

79. Ibid., p. 13.

80. Ibid., p. 33.

81. Mary Poovey, *Uneven Developments* (London, 1989), p. 17.

CHAPTER FIVE

A multiple vision 1988–9

A subtle article written by Nathalie Zemon Davis – and referred to briefly at the end of the first chapter in this book – was published in the *American Historical Review* in February of 1988.[1] Davis's focus was on historians of women, and on the 'historical community' which they formed in the process of their writing and their discussions with each other. She sought to place the histories of women being written by her contemporaries within a tradition. 'I want to consider how historians have conceptualized the body of historical knowledge and have placed their own life's work within it. I want to see how they maintained the rightful tension within their bosoms between the field that endures and their own brief embodiment of its claims . . .'. She uses as past exemplars one seventeenth, and two eighteenth-century historians – one of them a woman, Catherine Macaulay – and two historians-working in the first half of the twentieth: Marc Bloch and Eileen Power. In their 'feelings and struggles', she is sure that her fellow historians will have recognised 'the desire for rightful credit and indignation against thieves, the resentment of rivals and the appetite for renown . . .'. In order to practise a discipline which was 'committed to finding and making truthful sense of the past, they had to moderate these claims or at least put them to work for a higher cause. And so do we as well'. Zemon Davis searched for an image that she could give to history 'that would suggest the complexity, commitment, and multiple vision that I believe must be at its heart', and found one in Walter Benjamin's Angel of History. What she liked about it was that it had no sex, and it expressed 'the tension – between wholeness and fragmentation – and a multiple vision . . .'. But she wanted to add another body to the Angel, for her 'image of History would have at least two bodies in it, at least two persons arguing, always listening to the other as they gestured at their books; and it would be a film, not a still picture, so that you could see that sometimes they wept, sometimes they were astonished, sometimes they were knowing, and sometimes they laughed with delight'.

The late eighties was a period when history was indeed arguing, listening, gesturing; perhaps also weeping and feeling astonished. Historians of women welcomed diversity while at the same time expressing concern about the fragility of their position in the academic power structures. As historians of women grew in number, if not always in influence, differences in focus, sometimes in interpretation and to some extent in structural framework became increasingly visible. This chapter will look at a shift in the understanding of the term gender to a pivotal place in the approach of some historians of women who were influenced by the ideas of Foucault and Derrida. While a nineteenth-century historian of women such as Alex Owen felt liberated by this shift, an anxious note will later be heard from Judith Bennett, a medievalist who felt there was a threat to feminism contained within the shift away from the material lives of women towards a focus on 'gender as meaning'.[2] An article by French historians of women who did not feel that their discipline had made much impact again raised the issue of the danger of studying women's culture without a full recognition of the complex ways power was exercised within the wider social and political context. Another fruitful debate to which there was no easy resolution was stimulated by the interaction between literary criticism and history; that intercourse is the starting point for this chapter.

Mary Poovey is a literary critic whose study of 'the ideological work of gender in Mid-Victorian England' *Uneven Developments* was published in 1989.[3] In their interpretation of the construction of the middle class in *Family Fortunes*, Davidoff and Hall had moved, as they wrote, 'beyond the nineteenth-century inheritance of separate spheres', for they discovered that: 'Public was not really public and private not really private despite the potent imagery of "separate spheres". Both were ideological constructs with specific meaning which must be understood as products of a particular historical time.'[4] Their interest was in one particular historical time – 1780–1850 – and they 'attempted to draw a rounded picture of middle-class men and women as they followed their daily pursuits and carried on their individual lives . . .'.[5] Mary Poovey was not concerned with middle-class men and women as individuals: indeed, for her the concept of the individual was 'problematic'. One of the 'underlying points' of the book was 'that the ego-centred subject is a historical construct'.[6] Instead her focus is on what she termed '"border cases"' which had 'the potential to expose the artificiality of the binary logic that governed the Victorian symbolic economy'.[7] The cases vary from 'The medical treatment of Victorian women' and 'The social construction of Florence Nightingale', to 'The governess and Jane Eyre'.

The text – her book – that Poovey provided for her readers is, she wrote, 'closer to a fabric than a line of narration'.[8] In the opening chapter Poovey placed herself within the socially constructed production of knowledge, acknowledging that her choice of gender 'as a focus for analysis, is a function not of the absolute and ahistorical importance of gender, but of the coincidence between the importance this opposition held for mid-Victorian Britains and my own position as a white feminist within the Anglo-American academic establishment'.[9] In placing herself firmly within her own text, Poovey was avoiding what she described in an article also published in 1988 as the failure of deconstructive critics 'to examine the artifice – and historical specificity – of their own practice'.[10] As a result deconstruction tended to pose as 'an ahistorical master strategy', and outside of politics. So in order for deconstruction to be a sharp tool for feminist analysis 'deconstruction itself must be historicized and subjected to the same kind of scrutiny with which it has dismantled Western metaphysics'. In her article Poovey defended the method of deconstruction but also recognised a central problem for feminist historians in this method: 'To take deconstruction to its logical conclusion would be to argue that 'woman' is *only* a social construct that has no basis in nature . . . This renders the experience women have of themselves and the meaning of their social relations problematic to say the least . . .'. She defined the challenge 'for those of us who are convinced both that real historical women do exist and share certain experiences *and* that deconstruction's demystification of presence makes theoretical sense' as the need to work out some way to think both women and '"woman"'. She recognised it as no easy task. Feminists, Poovey advised, must both recognise that '"woman"' is 'a position within a dominant binary symbolic order' which is falsely unified, but also that 'there *are* concrete historical women whose differences reveal the inadequacy of this unified category in the present and the past'. Real historical women had been and continued to be oppressed, and the means of that oppression had to be analysed and fought. Feminists must, she argued, recognise that what 'women now share is a positional similarity that masqerades as a natural likeness'. It was this 'illusory similarity' which had 'historically underwritten oppression', and it must be willingly given up.

At the time Poovey's book and article appeared, the 'New Historicism' was emerging, in part as a reaction to what was seen as an exclusive poststructuralist focus on individual texts. Poovey identified the central assignment of the new historicism as an endeavour 'to historicise literary texts by relating them to the cultural scripts informing them'.[11] These 'cultural scripts' included institutions and events, and the project of new historicism, as its name implies, was a turn or return to history. However, as Judith Newton pointed out, 'the discipline of history is in some sense no longer there to be returned to, being itself in the process of moving on – toward literary criticism, post-structuralist discourse, and the text'.[12] This situation was apparent in a seminar held at Columbia Unversity in February 1988 where the principal speakers were Judith Walkowitz and two Professors of Literature.[13] The three speakers were very much in tune, living embodiment of the way 'literary and historical disciplines can free each other up'. As the introduction to the published edition of the discussion in *Radical History Review* (1989) put it, the 'exchange represents just one moment in an ongoing discussion among Anglo-American feminist theorists as they take account of post-structural literary criticism.' As a historian Judith Walkowitz directly addressed the challenge and the stimulus to historians of post-structuralism in the presentation of a central theme of her new project, *City of Dreadful Delight*. She stated early on in the paper that she was trying to 'map out a dense cultural grid through which conflicting and overlapping representations of sexual danger circulated'. Her attention to what she termed a 'cultural grid' moved her away from what literary critics termed 'intertextuality' – the juxtaposition of texts – to placing her texts within more material manifestations: 'social spaces, systems of communication, political and social networks'. She understood what she was engaged in as 'a dialogue with poststructuralist critics' in which she reformulated their insights to address topics conventionally of interest to the historian, such as power, human agency and experience. She cited Foucault for her understanding of power as 'a dispersed and decentered force that is hard to grasp and possess fully'. She also relied 'heavily on Foucault's insight into the discourse of sexuality as . . . an essential place to grasp the working of power in western societies'. This insight is, for Walkowitz, compatible with the insights of 'second-wave feminism', although she is critical of Foucault's failure 'to identify the dominant discourses on sexuality as male discourses'. As for the crucial issue for historians of agency, Walkowitz's perception was that men and women were makers of history, 'subjected to social and ideological constraints, yet forcefully resisting those same constraints'. Representations did not just reflect reality, but made things happen. Material reality existed as 'a destabilizing force on cultural production, forcing representations to be reworked'. To provide an orderly narrative of such a 'diachronic process', historians needed to find new narrative forms in their writing.

The two literary scholars at the seminar were more wary of what historians could lose in adopting the methods of another discipline. It was important, one of them warned, to recognise different sorts of narrative. The intention behind a historical narrative was to report facts: however ultimately elusive fact was, the intention of the historian produced a different narrative from that of the writer of fiction whose intention was to invent a story. The historian, all three speakers recognised, had traditionally been concerned with causality, with the answer to the question 'Why?'. This question seemed no longer to be viable from the linguistic perspective because it implied an objectivity outside language and thus an impossible position. 'Must representational analysis abandon inquiry into cause?' was the question left ultimately unanswered, although the speaker proposed during the discussion a meaning for 'Why?' which was 'to what effect', demanding no final explanation, but providing 'a recuperation of something which is in the realm of explanation'. The audience was reported as apparently 'unable to give up the notion – a notion each of the principal speakers had earlier tried resolutely to undermine – that historians deal with "facts" which somehow accord with the material world, and that neither the tools nor the texts of the literary critics can give access to that world'. The report found no resolution to the conflict, and also stated that Walkowitz's paper had called 'the whole enterprise of doing history into question'. In the discussion, Walkowitz professed herself 'more and more skeptical about the explanatory power of deep structures . . . I have focused increasingly on process . . . without assuming that a deep structural analysis of class, or indeed even gender, will tell me the answer . . .'.

A marked uncertainty about the traditional project of the historian was apparent in Walkowitz's paper; and a desire to defend that project in the reaction of the audience. One British historian shared neither Walkowitz's scepticism nor her audiences defensiveness. In her introduction to *The Darkened Room: Women, Power and Spiritualism in Late Victorian England*, Alex Owen wrote that although it was unwelcome in some quarters, for her, the 'acknowledgement of the historical narrative as nothing more nor less than a construction or a particular representation of the past has been a liberation'.[14] She stated that she had been 'particularly influenced by what some consider to be the twin theoretical devils: poststructuralism and psychoanalysis'. She believed that the 'recognition that the writing of history is a political act . . . is gaining ground', and hoped that her book would clearly represent 'an affirmation of the feminist historical agenda . . .'.[15] While she no longer saw the historian as 'an objective seeker after truth', she had retained her respect for 'the meticulous collection of material, scrupulous weighing of evidence, and conclusions backed by documentation . . .'.[16]

In the decade that followed, more historians of women were drawn to examine their acceptance of the validity of the traditional historical structures of material reality, agency and causality. Two books which would be markers of a new and assertive perspective on the possibilities inherent in abandoning old certainties were published in 1988. The first was Joan Scott's *Gender and the Politics of History* which was referred to in the last chapter, and the second *Am I That Name? Feminism and the Category of 'Women' in History* by a British writer, Denise Riley.[17] Riley wrote in her 'Acknowledgements' that the writing was made possible by American research fellowships, and that her 'overriding personal debt is to Joan Scott'. Riley's argument was that the collective term 'women' was innocent-sounding but troublesome: its apparent continuity could not be relied upon. Her aim was to demonstrate that '"women" is historically, discursively constructed, and always relatively to other categories which themselves change'. There was no stable site from which women could claim a collective identity. Riley was perhaps expecting an attack from those who felt that this position undermined the ground on which feminism stood, for she defended her position by claiming that far from evincing 'a glorious indifference to politics', she was proposing 'a thoroughly feminist undertaking' in recommending 'that all definitions of gender must be looked at with an eagle eye'.[18] Riley elaborated her thesis in chapters which focus on gendered understandings of the soul in Christian writings from the Middle Ages to the eighteenth century; the elision of the concept 'women' with 'the social' in the writings of nineteenth and early twentieth-century women, and the difficulties which faced suffragists who claimed that women were qualified for the vote through their 'psychic distinctiveness'.[19] In her final chapter, 'Bodies, identities, feminisms', she enlarged on her defence of the application of her ideas to contemporary political feminism. She found validation in Foucault's concept of effective history which contained the idea that not even the body is sufficiently stable concept to provide a reference point for 'women'. At the very end of the book, Riley asserted that 'feminism must be agile: it was enough to say, "Now we will be women . . ."' and admit 'a strategic willingness to clap one's feminist hand over one's theoretical mouth . . .'.[20]

Scott's book is longer than Riley's, and more rootedly historical. Frustrated at what she saw as 'the relatively limited impact women's history was having on historical studies generally', and needing to understand why this was happening, she had turned to theoretical issues in order to 'do feminist history'. Working within the existing parameters of the discipline of history had not altered the importance given to women's activities. Including women in historical categories such as 'working-class' neither changed the definitions of those categories nor ensured that women would not be excluded again. Women's history written from within the framework of social history, with its emphasis on 'experience', seemed to have ended up 'endorsing the ideas of unalterable sexual difference . . .'.[21] In some of the ideas of Derrida and Foucault, Scott found a 'radical epistemology' which could offer feminism the means to address epistemological questions, relativise the status of knowledge, link knowledge to power, and theorise the operations of difference.

She welcomed the shift – also endorsed by Judith Walkowitz – from study-ing origins to studying processes, especially the 'conflictual processes that establish meanings' and was undeterred by the destabilising of the concepts which were so commonly employed by historians: experience, identity, pol-itics.[22] For Scott, academic studies and feminism were part of the common project of confronting and changing existing distributions of power. She insisted that questions about gender would illuminate not only the history of relations between men and women but also all or most history, although the illumination could only be partial: she made no claim to 'total vision'.[23] Gender was knowledge about sexual difference which was historically specific, and analysing its variable and contradictory meanings would help the his-torian to understand the political processes by which those meanings were established. Defining knowledge, following Foucault, as 'the understanding produced by cultures and societies of human relationships', Scott argued that feminist history could become 'a way of critically understanding how history operates as a site of the production of gender and knowledge'.[24] She offered the essays which followed as a partial attempt at rethinking 'the history of politics and the politics of history'.[25]

The first essay is a re-working of the article Scott had contributed to *Past & Present* in 1983. In a new conclusion she estimated that the various approaches to women's history contained contradictions which had not prevented them from being productive: 'When put into dialogue with one another, these different approaches move the entire discussion forward.' However, this is only possible when 'the key terms of analysis are examined and redefined'. These terms are: woman as subject, gender and politics.[26] Scott then proceeded to examine 'gender' as 'a useful category of Historical Analysis' in the essay which first appeared in the *American Historical Review* and was summarised in the preceding chapter. The second part of the book contained two essays on gender and class, one of which was a response to E.P. Thompson's *The Making of the English Working Class*. The third part made use of Scott's own research in examining representations of women as workers in nineteenth-century France. The final part of the book explored ways out of the equality/difference dilemma: if historians em-phasised the collectivity of women, and thus difference from men, they were in danger of confirming the 'reality of separate spheres', whereas if they stressed equality, women's exclusion could be judged insignificant. Scott advocated the examination of the meanings of the terms used in specific historical contexts.

In Chapters Six and Seven, I will look at the continuing impact of Scott's challenge to women historians in the 1990s. Here I want to look at a debate which focused on the issues of culture and power and where the French participants acknowledged a debt to the ideas about power put forward by

Foucault. Inspired by the desire to draw together feminist historians from two traditions, an American historian whose work centred on French women provided in a forceful and concise article a framework for the achievement of 'an equitable world, a world in which women and men can be at once equal and different'.[27] Karen Offen called for feminists 'to draw on the most valuable features' of the historical traditions of Anglo-American and European scholars: the vision of equality should be combined with the reclaiming of the power of difference, 'of womanliness as women define it'. In her contribution to *Retrieving Women's History*, Michelle Perrot had asked of women's 'culture': 'is it a separate, independent culture, if not linked to distinctive sexual characteristics then at least to the historical fact of "gender"? Or is there simply a fluctuating division between the cultural practices of the sexes?' She had also identified the 'burning questions now-adays' as those concerned with power.[28] In 1986 an article with the title 'Culture et pouvoir des femmes' appeared in the French journal *Annales*: Perrot was joint author of this article with ten other French historians of women. An English edition appeared in the *Journal of Women's History* in the spring of 1989.[29] The authors began with a brief history of the development of women's history in France which provided a slightly different perspective from the outline offered by Michelle Perrot in *Retrieving Women's History*. It had taken off in 1970, 'helped along' by 'the feminist movement' – 'feminist activists were writing women's history before women historians themselves' – and the progress made by anthropology and the history of '*mentalités*'. The context in which the history of women was being written and studied in France was much less autonomous than in the US. The article's authors clearly still felt that they were, as Gerda Lerner had put it some years previously, an embattled lot, describing women's history as 'a task either tolerated or viewed as marginal by a discipline on which it has no direct impact'. Despite, or perhaps because of, the setting up in the mid-eighties of an official research body, and an ongoing colloquium, the authors detected a continuing fear that 'women's history might never become a spearhead for the discipline of history, or even a gadfly, because of its weaknesses'. These weaknesses were the preference for topics concerned with the body and sexuality; the 'continual use of the dialectic of domination/oppression which can scarcely get beyond a tautological statement'; too much use of 'prescriptive discourses'; a 'poor knowledge of the history of feminism and its connections with political and social history', and a 'lack of methodolo-gical and especially theoretical reflection'. Alongside these 'uncertainties', the authors tracked a development in 'the history of social and cultural repres-entations, and to a lesser degree, that of political representations' to which anthropology had contributed. Research on *roles sexuels* had moved in a new direction and had led to a sketching of the 'traits of a women's culture'.

The intention of the article was to examine this 'cultural approach to the sexes', and, with reference to particular studies, to 'propose a methodological analysis capable of revealing its contributions as well as its limitations'. They saw a danger in the formulation of women's power in a community as contained within particular cultural practices, for example those which are 'meant to help the entire community pass from birth to death'. This understanding could lead to a juxtaposition of male and female power in a way seen as complementary, 'forgetting that relations between the sexes are also fraught with violence and inequality'. The authors noted that the 'concept of complementarity' had been used widely in rural studies which had 'presented a world in equilibrium between men and women', a presentation which could erase 'the fact that the distribution of tasks has, after all, a positive and a negative pole and contains implicitly a hierarchical system'. Another danger when studying women's culture lay in an exclusive reliance on the anthropological meaning of culture: such studies could ignore women's position within 'the realm of intellectual activities' and avoid the need to look at the mechanisms by which they are excluded from this domain. The authors advocated a recognition that 'sexual division is never neutral', and a determination of the position of both sexes, 'since a value system based on division is not automatically based on equivalence'. They also argued that male domination should be treated as 'the expression of an unequal social relationship whose mechanism can be understood and whose characteristics, changing with time, can be analysed'. What was needed for an analysis of 'the subtle interplay of powers and counterpowers that constitute the secret web of the social fabric' was an approach such as that of Foucault which went 'beyond simplistic dichotomies and made possible a history of power – familial, social and political – viewed from the outside'.

In their final section, the authors pointed out that the affirmation that relations between the sexes were social contained the danger that the social and political were seen as oppositions, incorporating the distinction between the public and the private. Instead 'these two oppositions should perhaps be considered in conjunction with each other'. The understanding of 'this theoretical problem as particularly relevant to the history of women' constituted, they argued, 'in itself a new methodological approach'. They proposed that instead of 'underscoring women's absence from political life', there should take place a 're-evaluation, from a political perspective, of the various historical events in which women have taken part'. They acknowledged that such a proposal indicated a 'return to a concept of power that "crowns" the multiple powers which social scientists, since Michel Foucault and others, have sought to describe'. They defended this return as a 'necessary and salutary approach in a field of research where ambiguous use of the various meanings of *power* translates all too easily into a system of compensation'. Their proposal was that historians should analyse 'the causes and effects' of particular 'watersheds or ruptures' (terms they preferred to the notion 'event' which raised problems of long-term and short-term history) which involved women, whether directly or indirectly. The results they foresaw are the revelation of contradictions and paradoxes. For example, the granting of the right to vote to French women in 1944 was 'an addendum to a legislative bill that bore no direct relation to women's lives, it appears on the surface to have little or no connection with the feminist struggles which contributed to obtaining it'.

The French authors of this article share the determination of American historians to place 'women's culture' within a wider framework so that women were not isolated from what had always been considered as the main structures of power. At the same time they are reluctant to return to that traditional framework which was seen as a male construct. The same determination is apparent in an American study of French history which appeared in 1988: *Women in the Public Sphere in the Age of the French Revolution*.[30] For Joan Landes, the 'relation of women to the family and the economy cannot be well understood apart from the problematics of women and the public sphere'.[31] In her discussion of the 'incipient stages' of the development of women's movements in Western Europe and North America, Landes linked 'the shift in the organization of public life' from absolutism to bourgeois society to 'a radical transformation of the system of cultural representation'. Her proposition was that 'the collapse of the older patriarchy gave way to a more pervasive *gendering* of the public sphere'.[32] In her consideration of the public sphere, Landes made specific reference to the argument of Jurgen Habermas that 'the rise of a liberal democratic public sphere was central to the modernization of late eighteenth-century societies, but that commercialization, bureaucratization, and the "culture industry" progressively limited the scope for an autonomous public'.[33] She noted that Habermas had failed to reflect on 'what appear to be two crucial aspects of the formation of the modern public – the relation of the public sphere to women and to feminism'. Landes' argument is that 'the exclusion of women from the bourgeois public was not incidental but central to its incarnation'. There can be heard an echo of the thesis of *Family Fortunes* in her claim that 'the bougeois public is essentially, not just contingently, masculinist . . .'.[34]

A more direct 'Reply' to the challenge presented by the French historians of women by Lois Banner was published in the same issue of the *Journal of Women's History*.[35] Banner referred right at the start of her reply to a 'multifaceted critique of the "separate sphere" of women argument' among American historians, and specifically to the work of Carroll Smith-Rosenberg. The argument of the French authors would not, she averred, be a novelty to American historians, and their 'subtlety of exposition' would be welcome.

She admitted that the focus in the US, in contrast to Europe, was still largely on 'women as exclusive subjects', and that American historians 'have not fully faced the implications of the notion of power'. However, she admonished the authors of 'Culture et pouvoir' for the absence of a psychological dimension in their consideration of the concept of power. She then moved away from the French article to make intentionally provocative generalisations about 'that negativized male eros, that pornographic mentality, the controlling male gaze apparent in many major works of Western culture'. The readers she wishes to engage in her accusations about a Western culture characterised by male domination and violence are those involved in what she termed 'this "deconstructive enterprise"', which, despite its benefits, had allowed for the growth of a new men's studies denying implicitly the existence of patriarchy. She identified the 'perils of this analysis' in 'Culture et pouvoir des femmes' where she read 'the overriding message' to be the stressing of female power and the downplaying of masculine domination. What Banner feared was that in focusing mainly on women and giving them the position of agents of change, women's historians had 'allowed patriarchy to engage in that disappearing act at which it has been so adept'. American historians of women had entered the academy and 'climbed to the top of the academic hierarchy': she was afraid they might have adopted the existing models rather than overthrowing them. 'As we move to deconstruct the "woman-centred world" we have created in our histories over the past decade, we must be careful as to how and in what guise we put men back into it.' The guise she recognised was clearly a patriarchal one: her concern was that feminist history could disappear within 'an androcentric model of scholarship based on increasing complexity and detail'.

The relationship between feminism and the history of women was central to an article by Gisela Bock, a historian of twentieth-century Germany, in the first edition in the spring of 1989 of another new journal, *Gender and History*.[36] Bock acknowledged that women's history was 'influenced by feminist experience and thought, often by the desire to contribute to social change'. But she added that such motivation could also be 'a weakness, namely when today's ideas and values are simply projected back into the past, as an anachronism'. Bock was cautious in her assessment of the impact of women's history and women's historians on the historical profession; she described it as 'modest'. On the other hand, she gave a sense of the extent of the study of women's history in her references to the 'diversity of female experiences and situations which has been brought to light', and the fact that the discipline had used all methods and approaches available to historians. Bock's choice of approach was the by now widespread use of 'gender as a fundamental category of social, cultural and historical reality, perception and study'. She explained that using gender in this sense as a 'category' referred to 'an intellectual construct, a way of perceiving and studying people, an analytic tool that helps us to discover neglected areas of history'. The power of this tool was that it did not reduce history to a single model, but was a means to explore the variety and variability of the past. One section of Bock's article contained a critique of the dichotomous use of '"(biological) sex"' as opposed to '"(social) gender"', a critique thoroughly developed by Judith Butler.[37] Bock's main concern in the article was to emphasise the view that understanding women's history as gender history constituted the study of 'previously neglected relations between human beings and human groups'. She insisted on the importance of this perspective at a time when the 'concept of *gender* . . . threatens to become high fashion, which seeks to soften the challenge of women's history by developing a kind of gender-neutral discourse on gender'. Moreover, men, who could 'appear to exist beyond gender relations', needed to be brought into the discourse of gender. Studies which had revealed that gender was one form of legitimising power also contributed to awareness of the different forms of power. 'Looking at gender as a sociocultural relation enables us to see the links between gender and numerous other sociocultural relations in a fresh light; in addition to class there are, for example, race, age sexuality, culture, language, freedom, religion, family, economy.' She rejected the idea that there was a need to rank such relations, and did not claim that gender was more important than everything else, but pointed out that it was involved in all human relations.

An implicit response to Bock's article appeared in the same journal later that year. In it, Judith Bennett insisted that 'studying the historical intersection of race, class, gender, and other related factors' while 'they will take us far . . . will not bring moral and political vision back into women's history'.[38] Gisela Bock had hinted that her view of the concept of patriarchy was circumspect when she wrote that the relationship between men and women could not be reduced to 'a single and simple, uniform, primal or inherent cause or origin'.[39] In contrast, Judith Bennett, who had suggested that patriarchy might explain women's low status over a long period in a wide geographical area, put in a passionate plea for making 'patriarchy (and its mechanisms, its changes, its endurance) the central problem of women's history'.[40] Bennett's writings in the late eighties are central to the debates which were stirring among early modern and medieval historians. At first these debates focused on women's subordination and the possibility of a golden age when such subordination was absent, and later on the emergence of separate spheres. In 1987, Judith Bennett's first book, *Women in the Medieval Countryside: Gender and Household in Brigstock before the Plague* was published.[41] Although her title points to an awareness of the prevalent concern with gender, her introduction acknowledges no specific debt to feminism, and her focus is on the 'realities of women's lives' as interpreted through traditional historical sources.[42] She repudiated studies which had been based on 'a reading of the prescriptive advice found in literary, religious and statutory materials'. Her aim in the book was to add 'a medieval perspective to the history of working women in Europe', and to 'show how the choices that women faced in the seventeenth and nineteenth centuries were shaped not only by economic changes specific to those centuries, but also by enduring customs that had long limited female opportunities'.[43] She declared that she was challenging what became known as the 'Golden Age' assessment of the pre-industrial working experience of women implicit in the work of Alice Clark. She found 'ambivalences and contradictions' in the history of women in the medieval English countryside, but her final word was that the 'experience of women in Brigstock also demonstrates how enduring the subordination of women to men has been in "the history of England"'. That subordination was 'rooted in neither government nor economy, but rather in the household'.[44]

A book which followed on from Bennett's in both contemporary and historically chronological terms demonstrated the continuing focus of early modern historians on patriarchy, and raised the question of the timing of the emergence of separate spheres.[45] Susan Amussen's *An Ordered Society: Gender and Class in Early Modern England* also made reference to Alice Clark's work, but she followed up a different lead: Clark's insight into the relevance of the economic nature of the household to social relationships. Amussen pointed out that it was widely accepted that the early modern family was not only 'the fundamental economic unit of society, it also provided the basis for political and social order . . .'.[46] Her study traced the shift from a society which was ordered by this organic conception to one where 'a discussion of the family separate from other social instititutions becomes possible'.[47] She thus dated the division of society in to the public and the private in a period before industrialisation. Her study of gender is placed firmly within this wider framework: she identified differences in the experience of men and women, and she saw the family changing as the result of the changing economic activities of women: in wealthy families women were less economically active; in working-class families women's work was increasingly differentiated from men. This theme was an implicit challenge to *Family Fortunes*, where Davidoff and Hall had argued that this was a change which had occurred in the early nineteenth century. This subject was later taken up by Amanda Vickery in an article which linked the early modern to the nineteenth-century history of women.

The burying of the idea of a '"Golden Age" for women, a time when European women were not subordinated to and valued less than men', was acknowledged, somewhat regretfully, by Bonnie Anderson and Judith Zinsser in the introduction to *A History of Their Own*.[48] A strong challenge to the notion of such a 'bon vieux temps' for women, and the assertion of the durability of patriarchy was provided by Judith Bennett in a review essay of books on women in medieval and early modern Europe and Britain published in 1988.[49] Glancing at the work of historians such as Alice Clark and Eileen Power, she admitted that for 'contemporary historians, this image of a medieval (or preindustrial) golden age exercises a strong attraction'. Analysing what lay behind the durability of this perception, Bennett concluded that medievalists sought to overturn negative images of their period, while others found comfort in the notion that 'the worst aspects of sexual inequality – at least in economic terms – are comparatively modern and therefore neither profound nor enduring'. Current research did not sustain such a conception. Although she admitted that it was 'not easy to compare straightforwardly the working experiences of urban women between, say, 1200 and 1900', the studies she reviewed in the essay painted a picture 'of European women excluded, since at least the twelfth century, from full participation in their communities'. Bennett noted that historians were inclined to focus on change, but that women's work was an aspect of human existence that exhibited more continuity than change. Moreover, the verdict that 'many of the basic disadvantages faced by modern working women existed in medieval towns' suggested 'some of the standard explanations for women's subordination as workers – especially the dual villains of capitalism and industrialism – are incorrect'. What was needed was the identification of a feature common to the experience of women in a variety of environments over a long period: Bennett's choice is patriarchy. Women's work was controlled by men in both the private and the public spheres, and the two spheres intersected: advance in one would bring loss in the other. Her final paragraph gave advice to her fellow feminists who should be warned by the continuities she had described; to achieve economic equality, 'we must seek changes more profound and revolutionary' than affirmative action laws and legislation.

Judith Bennett's concerns about the directions taken by women's history were again passionately expressed in an article in *Gender & History*. Bennett's concern was that there was a 'trend towards increasingly less explicit feminist perspectives in our scholarship'.[50] She had been educated in Canada and was employed in the United States: like Scott and Bock, she acknowledged that over the previous twenty years, women's history had become a field of intense research, writing and teaching in the United States, but she argued that its place within the larger discipline was still ambivalent. Indeed, it had 'become an institutionalized part of many departments . . . at the cost of isolation and segregation'.[51] She also asserted that 'many historians of women have succumbed to pressures to produce studies that are palatable to their nonfeminist colleagues . . .'.[52] The newly launched *Journal of Women's History* 'never mentions feminist influence in women's history'.[53] Feminist theorists no longer drew 'significantly on the findings of historians of women', and 'the term "patriarchy" has all but disappeared from most women's history. Indeed, I was recently told that I could not use this word in the title of a collection of essays about medieval women because it might offend some readers'.[54] Turning to what she saw as the effort to achieve greater inclusivity by studying not merely women but also the 'intersection of race, class and gender', Bennett admitted that it had 'enhanced and deepened women's history', but it was often 'a politically correct compromise that accommodates the interests of the more powerful while excluding the more silent'.[55] She warned that 'the study of gender as advocated by Joan Scott and others must be pursued carefully and never in isolation from other feminist historical work'. She was afraid that a focus on 'a history of gender as meaning' would lead to the neglect of the 'material forces' which had shaped and constrained women's 'hard lives', and the way that women had coped with obstacles and challenges. She did not want historians of women to 'cut short their search for the meanings of gender', but she did want such studies to be combined with 'a return to feminism and to the grand feminist tradition of critiquing and opposing the oppression of women'.[56] She then traced – and refuted – attacks on the concept of patriarchy by feminist scholars among others, before developing her own vision of the return of the 'concept of patriarchy to the mainstream of feminist scholarship by studying its workings throughout history'.[57] The result, she averred, would be 'better history'; history that was analytical rather than descriptive, and history that addressed 'one of the greatest general problems of all history – the problem of the nature, sustenance, and endurance of power structures'.[58]

One of the questions posed by the authors of *A History of Their Own*, a two-volume narrative of the history of women from prehistory to the present, was why had women been seen as 'innately inferior' throughout history.[59] The growing body of research on the history of women and the demands of students combined to provide a strong impetus behind the writing of a book the purpose of which was to provide a synthesis of the work already done, and to shape their narrative around three questions: how had ordinary women lived; whether gender united all women, and the question about inferiority referred to above. They offered an answer to the second of these questions which is that the differences between women 'were outweighed by the similarities decreed by gender', and some explanation of the women's subordination as rooted in the family, and seen as part of the natural order.[60] The concept of patriarchy is not explicit in this explanation but it is certainly implicit. Their answer to the first question was limited by lack of information but their book did provide a valuable compilation of what was available at that time. Anderson and Zinsser were determined to place women at the centre and to reconceptualise European History. Their narrative placed a strong emphasis on the similarities in women's experience across national boundaries and the material was structured around the 'concepts of "place" and "function"', such as 'Women of the cities' and 'Women of the Fields'.[61] They found that as 'traditional historical periods and events receded in significance, others grew in importance'.[62] They identified factors crucial to women which had often been ignored in histories of men: contraception, clothing, diseases and the design of houses. Anderson and Zinsser cited Joan Kelly and Gerda Lerner's observations on the way history had both omitted women and distorted their lives by the way it was structured, and there is an echo of Lerner's voice in their assertion that women needed a history of themselves in order to achieve equality. The inclusion of women will result, they concluded, in 'a retelling of the human past enriched and made complete, a retelling that will give us for the first time a true history of humanity'.[63] This confident articulation of the task of historians of women was couched in the language of the seventies rather than the late eighties when the rhetoric was less certain and less comprehensive.

An even more ambitious and openly political meta-narrative was published in 1988. It contained a call for women to recognise that they had burst the bonds of patriarchal constraint, and I include it as an example of an assertive and populist strain in the writing of women's history. Rosamund Miles's *The Women's History of the World* is based on the idea that women's lives have been shaped by patriarchy, but her style is very different from Bennett's.[64] Rejecting any pretence of 'the traditional historical fiction of impartiality', her purpose is to 'assert the range, power and significance of women's contribution to the evolution of the human race, its huge variety in both the public and private spheres, and the massive female achievement on every level – cultural, commercial, domestic, emotional, social and sexual'.[65] The 'first step towards righting history's ancient and terrible wrongs', was, in her view, 'to accept the violence and brutality of men's systematic and sustained attack on the female sex . . .'. Her questions were how men did it, and how women let them get away with it. Echoing the observations of Mary Beard, she concluded that the 'final paradox of women's history' was that women had not 'ultimately been victims either of men or of history, but have emerged as strong, as survivors, as invincible'.[66] Thus Miles insouciantly sliced through the dilemmas which troubled more circumspect and academic historians.

'Real historical women have been (and are) oppressed, and the ways and means of that oppression need to be analyzed and fought.'[67] This was the confident and lucid voice of Mary Poovey in the article described at the beginning of this chapter. For Poovey, 'the project of deconstruction' would bring benefits to 'a feminism that is interested not only in the idea of "woman" but also in the concrete, class- and race-specific facts of historical women'.[68] The first of these benefits was the possibility of writing a history of how the contradictions in history over the definition of women had led to change: she cited the rights usually associated with men which opened to single women when the normative 'woman' was understood to be the married woman. The operations of power which divided the interests of women – for instance the fact that black women were subject to white women – could be revealed by 'deconstructing the term "woman" into a set of independent variables . . .'[69] Thirdly, dismantling binary thinking enabled historians to rethink the concept of power which lay behind the hierarchies implicit in such thinking. Analysis of the operations of power in society was possibly the most common focus of study for historians of women in the late eighties. Whether naming the structures of power which had dominated Western society since the Middle Ages patriarchy was fruitful was debated. There was widespread agreement on the use of gender – the relations between men and women – as a tool for such analysis, and a determination that a focus on gender should not exclude other relations of power nor exclude men from analysis. Beneath this general agreement there was some discomfort about the growing studies of culture where such studies seemed to ignore the presence of men's power, or misjudged the nature of the power wielded by women. A more particular historical debate was stirring about the shape of women's experience of work and the dating of the move towards separate spheres.

Notes and references

1. Natalie Zemon Davis, 'History's Two Bodies', *American Historical Review*, 93:1 (1988), pp. 1–31.

2. Judith Bennett, 'Feminism and history', *Gender & History*, 1:3 (1989), p. 259.

3. Mary Poovey, *Uneven Developments* (London, 1989).

4. Leonore Davidoff and Catherine Hall, *Family Fortunes* (London, 1987), p. 33.

5. Ibid., p. 35.

6. Poovey (1989), p. 20.

7. Ibid., p. 12.

8. Ibid., p. 20.

9. Ibid., p. 23.

10. Mary Poovey, 'Feminism and deconstruction', *Feminist Studies*, 14:1 (Spring, 1988), pp. 52–65.

11. Poovey (1989), p. 23.

12. Judith Newton, 'Dialogue', *Journal of Women's History*, 2:3 (Winter, 1991), p. 102.

13. Judith Walkowitz *et al.*, 'Patrolling the borders of feminist historiography and the new historicism', *Radical History Review*, 43 (1989), pp. 23–43.

14. Alex Owen, *The Darkened Room: Women, Power and Spiritualism in Late Victorian England* (London, 1989), p. xi.

15. Ibid.

16. Ibid., p. x.

17. Joan Wallach Scott, *Gender and the Politics of History* (New York, 1988); Denise Riley, *'Am I that Name?' Feminism and the Category of 'Women' in History* (London, 1988).

18. Riley (1988), pp. 1–2.

19. Ibid., p. 94.

20. Ibid., p. 113.

21. Scott (1988), pp. 3–4.

22. Ibid., p. 3.

23. Ibid., p. 10.

24. Ibid., pp. 2, 10.

25. Ibid, p. 11.

26. Ibid., p. 24.

27. Karen Offen, 'A historically based definition of feminism', *Signs*, 14 (Autumn, 1988), pp. 149–7.

28. S. Jay Kleinberg, ed., *Retrieving Women's History* (Oxford, New York, 1988), p. 56.

29. Cecile Dauphin, Arlette Farge *et al.*, 'Women's culture and women's power: issues in French women's history', *Journal of Women's History*, 1:1 (Spring, 1989), pp. 63–88.

30. Joan Landes, *Women in the Public Sphere in the Age of Revolution* (Ithaca, NY, 1988).

31. Ibid., p. 7.

32. Ibid., p. 2.

33. Ibid., p. 5.

34. Ibid., p. 7.

35. Lois Banner, 'A reply to "Culture et pouvoir" from the perspective of United States women's history', *Journal of Women's History*, 1:1 (Spring, 1989), pp. 101–7.

36. Gisela Bock, 'Women's history and gender history: aspects of an international debate', *Gender & History*, 1:1 (Spring, 1989), pp. 7–30.

37. Judith Butler, *Gender Trouble: Feminism and the Subversion of Identity* (London, 1990).

38. Judith Bennett, 'Feminism and history', *Gender & History*, 1:3 (Autumn, 1989), pp. 251–71.

39. Bock (1989), p. 11.

40. Bennett (1989), p. 266.

41. Judith Bennett, *Women in the Medieval Countryside: Gender and Household in Brigstock before the Plague* (Oxford, 1987).

42. Ibid., p. 5.

43. Ibid., p. 4.

44. Ibid., p. 198.

45. Susan Amussen, *An Ordered Society: Gender and Class in Early Modern England* (Oxford and New York, 1988).

46. Ibid., p. 2.

47. Ibid., p. 188.

48. Bonnie Anderson and Judith Zinsser, *A History of Their Own* (London, 1988), p. xxii.

49. Judith Bennett, '"History that stands still": women's work in the European past', *Feminist Studies*, 14:2 (Summer, 1988), pp. 269–83.

50. Bennett (1989), p. 252.

51. Ibid.

52. Ibid., p. 253.

53. Ibid., p. 255.

54. Ibid., p. 254.

55. Ibid., p. 257.

56. Ibid., p. 259.

57. Ibid., pp. 262–3.

58. Ibid., p. 266.

59. Anderson and Zinsser (1988), p. xiv.

60. Ibid., p. xv.

61. Ibid., pp. xviii–xix.

62. Ibid., p. xix.

63. Ibid., p. xxiii.

64. Rosamund Miles, *The Women's History of the World* (London, 1988).

65. Ibid., pp. xv, xi.

66. Ibid., p. xiv.

67. Poovey (1988), p. 62.

68. Ibid., p. 57.

69. Ibid., p. 59.

CHAPTER SIX

Writing inside the kaleidoscope 1990–3

In an article in *Gender & History*, Kali Israel echoed and expanded Sheila Rowbotham's use of the image of the kaleidoscope to suggest some of the complexities of 'seeing' women historically.[1] 'Through the eyepiece of a kaleidoscope, one sees a multitude of fragments, forming patterns that shift with the movement of the viewer. Further, each fragment of the pattern is a tiny mirror, catching the colours and images of the "outer" world and re-representing them, in a space in which each mirror also echoes each other mirror.' Israel recognised the limitations of this metaphor to be the inability of the historian, unlike the viewer, to 'look at real objects without reflection, refraction or distortion'. Instead, he or she had to write from inside the kaleidoscope. Israel did not deny the existence of a 'reality' in the past, but asked historians to 'admit the impossibility of living and writing outside of representation'. This perception of the complexity of the task of the historian of women and her positioning within the kaleidoscope is a hallmark of the writings of the nineties. Mary Poovey's assurance that historians could make use of the insights of poststructuralism while totally abandoning neither the traditional framework of the historian nor a feminist politics was described in the last chapter. In this chapter I will begin by looking at the thinking of others similarly motivated. The dimensions of a feminist critique of post-structuralist theories as far as they impinge on the writing of gender and women's history were emerging. Another critique, that of the ethnocentrism of the writing of the histories of women in the West, brought race firmly on to the agenda. This project was linked to the tensions between the particular histories of women and the more general framework implicit in a feminist perspective, and in the use of the concept patriarchy.

The nineties opened with an exchange between two American historians who can be seen to embody two different perspectives on the writing of history. The articulation of conflicting views was contained within mutual reviews of the books they had published in 1988: *Heroes of Their Own Lives: The Politics and History of Family Violence* by Linda Gordon; *Gender and the Politics of History* by Joan Scott.[2] The crux of the exchange was, as Gordon put it, Scott's challenge to the idea that a historian can make a 'distinction between the representation of events and the physical experience of them'. In her review, Scott maintained that Gordon's argument contained contradictions between the social control framework, which she adopted, and her determination that the women in her study who were subject to violence were autonomous agents. She suggested that these contradictions might have been avoided had Gordon understood agency 'not as an attribute or trait inhering in the will of the autonomous individual subjects, but as a discursive effect, in this case the effect of social workers' constructions of families, gender, and family violence'. In her reply Gordon challenged this understanding of agency as 'an effect', arguing that it 'drains that notion of any meaning'. She pointed out that her reason for using the concept of social control was its 'explanatory power', and that her interpretation sought to complicate it. In her review of Scott's book, Gordon suggested that Scott was trying to push all historians of women into one mould, while in fact Scott's own essays demonstrated that deconstructionism was not the only source of her strength as a historian. Gordon welcomed deconstructionist lines of enquiry which led to 'rewarding and subversive challenges to lazy and status quo readings of experience', but she remained cautious about what could be claimed for the method. In particular she was concerned about what she saw as 'a removal of the gaze from power'. Scott read Gordon's position as a resistance to poststructuralist theory. But she then suggested that such resistance might be a sign of the vitality of feminism: the two historians retained their respect for the other's position.

Another judicious review of Scott's book, together with Denise Riley's *Am I That Name?* was written for *Gender & History* by Catherine Hall.[3] She admitted to having put off the writing of the review: 'The books have sat in a pile just by my desk, had coffee spilt on them, been written on, carried around with me . . . and generally occupied an uncomfortable space somewhere between my conscious and unconscious self . . .'. She attributed this reluctance to the resistance to theory of British historians in particular, and to the fundamental challenge which Scott and Riley presented to the established frameworks. Hall sees Riley as 'operating on the borderlands between philosophy and history', and Scott as 'firmly located within history' and thus more challenging. She admired Scott's skill as demonstrated in those essays in the book which are historical studies, commenting that she could not help thinking – like Linda Gordon – that Scott was 'engaging in practices under the name of post-structuralism which have long been the stock-in-trade of critical social history'. She claimed that the use of gender as an analytical term was a feminist insight, as was the perception attributed to Foucault of power as operating on many sites. She maintained that the most sustained critique of essentialist ideas about women – the direction of Riley's argument – had come not from poststructuralism but from the work of black women in the United States and Britain. A central concern which remained with Hall was the question of subjectivity, and the vital and connected issues of 'structure and agency'. The excision of the autonomous individual (seen by poststructuralists as an illusion) results for Hall in 'a curious loss of feeling in historical writing'. She wanted to retain the process of identification with the historical subject without which it is not possible to 'imaginatively evoke difference, the difference of other worlds and times . . .'. Alongside an awareness of 'the discursive fields which construct meaning'. she called for 'an emphasis on "we" acting, on us being present and active in our own making'. In the end Hall is 'left wanting to hold on to' many of the arguments put forward by Riley and Scott, but without their certainties.

The shift by some historians of women towards poststructuralism was thus finding a circumspect response and one which suggested that its ideas were not as radical nor as new as its practitioners asserted. There was also a determination to retain aspects of the historian's claims to knowledge which were apparently under threat. Issue 13 of *The Women's Studies International Forum* in 1990 was devoted to 'British Feminist Histories' and was edited by Liz Stanley. In her introduction, Stanley acknowledged that feminism was not a unitary category, and that 'the category Women is multiply fractured by difference on grounds of class, race and ethnicity, sexuality, age, and dis/able-bodiedness'.[4] She also identified within the papers in the volume she had edited 'a hint . . . that rather than seeing feminist history as the recovery of all the pieces of a jigsaw puzzle, such that we finally gain a single, complete, and unseamed picture of the whole . . . that there is no "whole" piece together, but rather contiguous though clashing, and certainly not seamlessly meshing, *competing histories*'. This understanding was accompanied by a defence of history against 'deconstructionism' in Liz Stanley's own contribution to the collection.[5] She looked in particular at Denise Riley's 'speculative deliberation on the category of *women* in history', and, although she welcomed the recognition of 'the ontological experience of *women* as shaky', she wanted to retain the ability to take a feminist position based on a 'minded choice', albeit one that was only preferable, not absolute. She concluded her article with an examination of the understandings of herself as a woman expressed by the Victorian servant Hannah Cullwick in her diaries. Stanley used this analysis as a demonstration of the importance of admitting that 'the complexities of the categories *women* and *men* are not reserved knowledge for theoreticians/researchers . . .'.

A third British historian of women offered a considered response to poststructuralist ideas in a collection of essays international in scope: *Writing Women's History: International Perspectives* (1991) was edited by an American, a Canadian and a British historian (Karen Offen, Ruth Roach Pierson and Jane Rendall) and included essays by French historians ('Culture et pouvoir', discussed in the Chapter Five), and one by Gisela Bock.[6] Jane Rendall's contribution to the volume referred to the shift of focus in the 1980s from the causes of sexual difference to its meaning. But she warned that in order to study change historians needed to 'supplement the new skills of the reading of meaning with older historical practice'.[7] Traditional archival sources such as court records and censuses, and the material culture needed to be examined as well as the more literary products. Her article began by tracing two roots of the discipline of women's history in the UK: the new approaches to social history and the work of feminist historians, and she judged there to be a marked contrast between the work that had emerged from these impulses. Turning to 'the emergence of gender as a primary category of historical analysis' which she traced back to the theoretical writings of Joan Kelly and Nathalie Zemon Davis in the 1970s, she welcomed the use of the term 'gender' as a 'means by which to examine all historical social relationships from a feminist perspective: this includes the study of male institutions and the construction of masculinity'.[8] She repeated Nathalie Zemon Davis's demand in her *History Today* article that masculinity needed to be deconstructed. Rendall also appreciated the way awareness of gender had 'already offered us the benefit of an interdisciplinary perspective'. She noted the consideration by historians of 'language, symbol, form and the challenge of the subjective', and the influence of Foucault in the furthering of 'the understanding of gendered political structures through arguments shaped by structuralism and poststructuralism'.[9] She acknowledged the benefits of such approaches in the writings of Lyndal Roper, Mary Poovey, Joan Scott and Denise Riley. However, she then went on to identify two reservations of feminists – including herself in this designation – of focusing on the history of gender. Study of discourse could mean an undue emphasis on the history of the literate and the powerful. The second reservation was the need to continue to write the history of women who had so far been neglected, such as black women in Britain. Liz Stanley had also called for attention to be paid to differences between women, and Rendall added a plea for 'an end to the now ritual invocation of "and black women" as the only difference seen but which actually goes no further than a formula of words that leaves untouched actual relations of power . . .'.[10]

Gisela Bock's article in *Writing Women's History: International Perspectives* examined and challenged the dichotomies in which gender relations had been studied over the previous 20 years. The first three – nature/culture, work/family, public/private – had, she argued, 'been taken up and used as crucial conceptual frameworks in the newly emerging women's history of the past decades'.[11] They had also been challenged as expressions of gender difference, and reconstructed as contrary distinctions, which were neither mutually exclusive – they could co-exist – nor hierarchical. But one of the results of 'the attempts to resolve the earlier binary modes with the help of new concepts and theoretical frameworks' had been the emergence of new dichotomies: sex/gender; equality/difference; integration/autonomy ('of women's studies in respect to scholarship at large, and of women in respect to academic institutions'). These new dichotomies reflected 'the increasingly complex character of the categories under which gender relations are being considered and studied'.[12] The challenge was to dismantle, historicise and deconstruct the given meanings of these categories, for example by claiming '"equality in difference"' and '"difference in equality"'.[13]

Gisela Bock's theoretical writing in this essay and in her article in *Gender & History* which was summarised in Chapter Five, provided one of two perspectives used for comparison by a Dutch historian, Mineke Bosch.[14] Bosch was finding that 'every reference to theory in women's history is to gender and with reference to gender is to the theoretical formulations of Scott'. Bosch compared what she saw as Scott's ambitious aim of developing 'a more or less all-encompassing proposal for the use of gender as an analytic category', with Bock's recommendation that historians of women 'rethink their constructions and categories'. She welcomed Bock's refusal to choose between gender and women's history, and found Bock 'less coercive'. Bosch read in Scott's advocacy of 'a univocal new approach . . . the compelling vocabulary of scientific progress', accompanied by a depreciation of what went before. Bosch was concerned that a serious consequence of adhering 'to one theoretical formulation . . . is the exclusion of other theoretical issues and debates'. Like Liz Stanley, she was conscious that historians made choices, and suggested that 'we should strive for another common language in which there is room for multiple voices, which recognizes multiple interests in writing women's history and does not aim at too narrow a programme or too broad generalization'.

Another call for a 'historical practice' which 'could combine the concerns of historians of women and historians of gender' came from an article by Louise Newman in *The Journal of Women's History* published in the winter of the same year, 1991.[15] Newman critically examined Linda Gordon's desire (expressed in a chapter published in 1986 and described in Chapter Four) to find 'a balance between accuracy and mythic power'. Gordon had identified two purposes in writing women's history, one of which was based on the claim that there whereas there was no objective truth within reach of the historian, 'there are degrees of accuracy; there are better and worse pieces of history'. The other was aimed at 'mythic power', the writing of history with the intention of achieving political change. Newman was unhappy with the implicit assumption in both such approaches that historians had access to the experience of people in the past through 'vestiges of evidence', and that the histories they wrote could be assessed 'in terms of their "accuracy" in relation to evidence'. She compared Gordon's formulation of history as 'a more or less accurate account of recoverable experiences' to Joan Scott's understanding of history as the *representation that constructs experience* (italics in original). For Scott, what a historian is doing is not relating experiences previously unknown but 'giving new meaning to experiences never before understood in such a way'. Newman sees the two approaches as categorising historians of women in the first case, and gender historians in the second: 'representations play an analogous role for historians of gender as the category of experience does for historians of women'. While she accepted that 'the perspective afforded by poststructuralist theories no longer enables us to think of women's history as an accurate reconstruction of objective experiences', she did not wish to 'give up on the project of writing the history of women's experiences'. The possibility of doing this could, she argued, be provided by a redefinition of the term experience to that which is '*produced by* and *mediated through* cultural forms'. For Newman this would not involve a total rejection of the material, nor of agency. She cited Mary Poovey's view that although '"texts" are the only form of reality', the conditions that produce the texts, and the people who are the subjects of those texts are '*material in the ever elusive last instance*' (italics in Newman).[16] For Poovey, that which is material does remain elusive because it can only be known through representations. It seems that Newman was seeking to retain the political edge of the scholarly endeavour she was examining, through a commitment to 'a kind of agency that retains some relationship between experience and representation, between people and power'. Using the example of a feminist discourse in 1913 she argued that the historian of gender would ask questions about '*how* this particular feminist discourse of 1913 was produced, *why* it emerged when it did, and *where* and *in what cultural forms* it was represented'. It is within these questions that she believed human agency is restored to the framework.

Newman had made reference to Joan Scott's understanding of history as 'constructing' experience, and Scott's controversial position will shortly be examined in more detail. Ruth Roach Pierson, a Canadian historian and one of the editors of *Writing Women's History: International Perspectives*, agreed with Scott that the concept needed to be 'problematised'.[17] Her concern in the contribution she made to the volume was with a particular misuse of the term. It was one, she pointed out, which had been used by feminist historians to challenge the universality of the ' "grand narratives" ' of western history.[18] In their struggle for legitimation they had called attention to the differences between men's and women's experience, a difference which was part of a power relationship. The danger was that a historian concerned to emphasise the experience of oppression of women in the past could use her power to misrepresent that experience. Examining a study of women's involvement in the fur trade in Canada, Pierson applauded 'the reconstitution of the society and economy of the fur trade and the recovery of Native women's indispensable place within it', but she cast doubt on the author's 'attempt to resurrect the interior experience of women whose specific experience of oppression Van Kirk does not share and for which no written records in their own voices exist'.[19] In her essay Roach Pierson made a preliminary attempt to problematise the concept of experience, placing the writing of women's historians within the context of their own experience of subjugation and of oppression in their struggle to create a space for themselves. Her voice chimed in with those by Liz Stanley and Catherine Hall in calling upon historians of women to 'be prepared to listen with humility to the "voices of experience" of those different from ourselves and, most especially, of those vis-à-vis whom we stand in a relation of dominance'.[20]

Roach Pierson had focused on one dilemma arising from the use of 'the conception of experience' which she understood as lying 'at the intersection of theory and practice in women's writing'. In an essay in the collection *Feminists Theorize the Political*, Joan Scott advocated recognition of the fact that 'what counts as experience is neither self-evident nor straightforward', and that its meaning was contested and therefore political.[21] Experience was not, in her understanding, 'the origins of our explanation, not the authoritative (because seen or felt) evidence that grounds what is known'. Rather, it was 'that which we seek to explain, that about which knowledge is produced'.[22] Scott did not seek to abandon the use of the word, which was ubiquitous and deeply embedded in historian's narratives. But she did wish historians to abandon the premise that there was ever an 'unmediated relationship between words and things', and to work with the idea that experience 'is at once always an interpretation and is in need of interpretation'.[23] Scott also implicitly responded to her critics when she denied that the understanding of subjective identity as 'a discursive event' meant that subjects were deprived of agency. An essay by Judith Butler in the same volume extended this claim when she asserted: 'the constituted character of the subject is the very precondition of its agency'.[24] Butler was a professor of Humanities at Johns Hopkins, and her argument had been presented in an extended version in *Gender Trouble*.[25] There she had explored 'what political possibilities are the consequence of a radical critique of the categories of identity'.[26] To undermine the category 'women', she argued, did not mean that women were no longer agents. Indeed, the assertion of the feminist 'we' always excluded some women. She argued instead that identity was not a prelude to political action, but that politics was to be found in the very process of establishing and regulating identity. Whereas the assertion of a feminist viewpoint fixed and constrained those whom it sought to liberate, the desconstruction of identity allowed for the challenge to the binarism of sex, and the acceptance of a greater range of political possibilities. In her article in *Feminists Theorize the Political*, Butler explained that deconstruction did not involve negation or dismissal, but led to an opening up and loosening of the deployment of a term or category. She accepted the 'political necessity to speak as and for *women*', and sought to 'release the term', to allow it many meanings.[27]

The implications of the poststructuralist critique of subjectivity and historical agency, and the relationship of the analytical categories of discourse and experience was the focus of an article by an historian of German women, Kathleen Canning.[28] Canning was aware of the anxiety that feminist inquiry might lose its critical edge faced with 'the sense of identities and subjectivities fracturing, of categories and concepts dissolving in a "new master-narrative" of multiplicity, fluidity, and interdeterminacy'. She repeated the view expressed by Catherine Hall that it was important for feminist historians to recognise that while the debates had centred on the writings of Foucault, Lacan and Derrida, feminist history had already 'destabilized the historical canon of social history *before* their works became widely known among historians'. In rejecting the idea that biological essentialism provided an explanation of gender inequality, feminist historians had revealed the power of 'language and discourse to socially construct these inequalities and to anchor them in social practices and institutions'. Turning to Joan Scott's writings, Canning agreed with Bock that new binary oppositions had appeared in which one of the pair – in the case of discourse and experience, the former – 'always seems to determine or construct the other . . .'. In rejecting the appeal to experience for its obscuring of 'the workings of the ideological system', Canning argued that Scott constructed oppositional categories where there could be 'complementary historical tasks' in the analysis of 'how difference . . . was constituted and the exploration of how that difference was experienced by women in specific historical settings'. Scott's oppositional constructions were particularly problematic for historians of modern Germany where responsibility for the policies of the Third Reich, and in particular the Holocaust, provided a particularly sensitive domain for 'delineating the boundaries between agency (responsibility) and victimization'. This example illustrated, in Canning's view, 'the historical specificity of our theoretical problems', and thus the mutability of the dilemmas in feminist history. Canning joined her fellow historians of women in ending on an optimistic note, celebrating the 'richness and diversity of feminist history in the United States' in a moment when 'fragmentation, destabilization, and even deconstruction' were fruitful.

A rather more acute discomfort with what she understood as the displacement of women's history by gender history was expressed by a German historian in a collection of essays on Women's Studies published in 1993.[29] Uta Schmidt described two aspects of her own experience which were the starting points of her interest in theory. When giving seminars about her research on the medieval French writer Christine de Pizan, she had 'realised with a certain horror that . . . de Pizan was understood not in her own context but in that of the present day. She was transformed into a single working mother involved in feminist writing'.[30] She also confessed to a tendency to keep quiet about her feminist views of history when talking to her male colleagues for fear of being regarded as 'anti-men'. The resulting contradictions between her thinking as a historian and her life as a feminist she sought to resolve by grappling with the issue of partisanship in writing history. She saw her article as contributing towards the revitalisation of the theoretical discussions in which feminist thought needed to participate. The central question she was faced with was 'how a feminist perspective can be valid both in terms of women's experiences and interests, past and present, and in terms of the scholarly, scientific character of historical research and learning'. There are echoes here of the division which Linda Gordon had outlined between histories which sought mythic power, and histories which pursue accuracy. Schmidt made it clear that she was not looking for a particular feminist methodology: in her view a 'feminist perspective uses all the methods and approaches available to historians'. For her, 'the originality of the feminist perspective lies in the particular links made by feminist historians between their contemporary views of the human past and the historical evidence provided by the sources'.[31] She identified two paths which feminist historians were taking and which she thought they should avoid. One was to use gender as a category of analysis: this approach, she suggested, had led to validity being dependent on 'the extent to which feminist engagement disappears'. The other was partisanship, where validity was to be found the 'readiness of women to identify with suffering and oppression and to take a supportive partisan view of the oppressed'.[32] The weakness of this approach was that concepts such as 'female consciousness' and 'oppression' remained unexamined, and uncomfortable facts such as the active participation of women in totalitarian regimes were ignored. Her solution to these dilemmas was consciously to combine objectivity with partisanship: indeed, she asserted that partisan and objective elements were both present in historical scholarship and understanding, and each required the other in order to exist. She advocated 'an ongoing complex self-reflectivity' about the historian herself, about the historical material, about the 'conceptual or political choices which shape ones way of thinking about history', and about how far what the historian wrote would contribute to the demise of patriarchy.[33] This essay is reminiscent of the arguments put forward by Judith Bennett and described in Chapter Five, although here there is a more comfortable sense of a resolution to a dilemma having been found.

Historians of women were succeeding in developing individual approaches which welcomed some aspects of poststructuralist thinking, yet retained both a feminist edge and the acceptance of the material and the agency of women as valid concepts. The opening paragraphs of an introduction by Catherine Hall to a collection of her own essays, *White, Male and Middle-class* bear witness to her acceptance of the efficacy of poststructuralist ideas: 'Historians construct stories, stories which necessarily have a narrative shape but in which the tensions between the teller, the tropes of the discourse (the beginning, the middle and the end), and what are understood to have been the events, are consciously worked on.' But she added firmly that for her, 'history . . . is not just another fiction. Historical research is always premised on a relationship between past and present, is always about investigating the past through the concerns of the present, and always to do with in-terpretation'.[34] Implicit in this understanding of the historian's task is a rejection of what she refers to later in the essay as Scott and Riley's 'refusal of "the real"', although she presents their arguments without explicitly rejecting them.[35] In the final section of the introduction, Hall states that feminist history 'has moved a long way', and that its 'object of study is no longer women, if indeed it ever was, but its forms of analysis are distinct-ively feminist. It takes gender as one, but not the only, crucial axis of power'.[36] She also called attention to the continued marginality of her dis-cipline when she observed that the 'professional development of feminist history has been horribly skewed by the refusal of the British historical establishment to recognize it', citing an article published in 1987 by David Cannadine which offered a critique of the work of British historians but failed to 'mention feminism in his consideration of a possible future for British history'. Nevertheless, Hall finished this opening chapter with an optimistic view of the 'productive terrain' of the margins.[37]

From this marginal space there had grown an understanding of 'the ways in which the margins are determining of the centre' in the work of those who had challenged the ethnocentrism of feminist historians, including – belatedly, she acknowledged – Hall herself.[38] She paid tribute to Anna Davin's article 'Imperialism and Motherhood' as an exception to the rule that British feminist historians were at first obtuse on questions of race.[39]

Criticisms of the disregard of the 'fundamental ways in which white women have benefited from the oppression of Black people' became increasingly common in the 1980s, and there was a fruitful response to it.[40] This criticism tuned in with the call for a less rigid framework for the study of women in history, and it came often from historians concerned with the margins, with subaltern history. Valerie Amos and Pratibha Parmar identified the task of beginning to identify 'the ways in which a particular tradition, white Ethnocentric and Western, has sought to establish itself as the only legitimate feminism in current political practice'.[41] Elsa Barkley Brown, who taught both in a history department and at a centre for Afro-American and African Studies, pointed out that historians of women were prepared to 'recognize how black women's life choices have been constrained by race', but were 'less apt to acknowledge, that is to make explicit and to analyze, . . . how white women's lives are also shaped by race'.[42] She called for the acceptance of history as a process where 'everybody is talking at once': it was not like a well-orchestrated and firmly conducted classical musical score, but like jazz, always challenging, always surprising, and where issues are not settled, nor conversations ended.

The view that in the early nineties white feminist scholars were still only paying 'lip service to race as they continue to analyse their own experience in ever more sophisticated forms', was expressed by Evelyn Brooks Higginbotham in an article in *Signs*.[43] She cited Elizabeth Spelman as pointing out that white feminists failed 'to separate their whiteness from their womanness', while discerning 'two separate identities for black women, the racial and the gender', and concluding 'that the gender identity of black women is the same as their own'. On the contrary, Higginbotham argued, gender was deeply coloured by race, and a black and a white woman's identity 'was reconstructed and represented in very different, indeed antagonistic, racialized contexts'. One result of this, she suggested, was that Black women historians were reluctant to analyse gender 'along the lines of the male/female dichotomy so prevalent among white feminists'. She accepted that it was also true that gender conflict had been ignored by Black women because of 'the totalizing tendency of race'. Race was 'an unstable, shifting and strategic reconstruction' and feminist scholars should recognize it as such. 'We must bring to light and to coherence the one and the many that we always were in history and still actually are today', she declared. Only a year later, another American historian of women, who had 'once lamented that the historical experiences of Black women had been neglected, obscured, distorted, or relegated to the back pages of our collective consciousness', proclaimed that 'such is not the case today'.[44] Darlene Clark Hine was nevertheless concerned about the 'paucity of sustained analysis on the overwhelming poverty of the vast majority of Black women', and the resulting myth of the 'heroic, transcendent Black woman able to do the impossible . . .'. She also wanted black historians to write about white women and vice versa. Her motivations were consciously involved with the contemporary: such ' "crossover history" ' would, she believed, lead to 'progress in the war against sexism, racism and class oppression'.

In the early nineties, other historians of women examined the way gender was implicated in the structures of colonial authority. Ann Stoler asked: 'in what ways were gender inequalities essential to the structure of colonial racism and imperial authority? Was the strident misogyny of imperial thinkers and colonial agents a by-product of received metropolitan values, a reaction to contemporary feminist demands in Europe, or a novel and pragmatic response to the conditions of conquest? Was the assertion of European supremacy in terms of patriotic manhood and racial virility an expression of imperial domination or a defining feature of it?'[45] Stoler raised these questions in a study of 'the ways in which imperial authority and racial distinctions were fundamentally structured in gender terms'. Her wide-ranging research into the practices of European Asian colonies from the seventeenth to the twentieth century suggested to her 'that sexual control was both an instrumental image for the body politic, a salient part standing for the whole, and itself fundamental to how racial policies were secured and how colonial projects were carried out'.[46] Vron Ware used different material – the impact of the arguments of Ida B. Wells, an Afro-American who toured Britain in the 1890s – to examine the ways in which 'conflicting definitions of female sexuality and thus of femininity were inextricably tied to ideologies of race and class'.[47] Ware had become conscious of how the insularity of British women's history was 'a key to understanding the way that racism had been separated from gender relations in contemporary analysis'. She was also led through her research to an understanding of how gender 'played a crucial role in organizing ideas of "race" and "civilization" . . .'[48]

A similar perspective was developed by Tessa Liu in an article published in the same year in an article in *Women's Studies International Forum*.[49] Liu 'sketched with broad strokes very complex and nuanced social situtations in the hope of capturing simple patterns that have been overlooked'. She suggested that race was a widespread principle of social organisation related to kinship and bloodlines and thus to gender: 'Considered in these terms, race as a social category functions through controlling sexuality and sexual behaviour'. She cited Gisela Bock's work on women's productive rights in Nazi Germany as a revelation of the taking of assumptions about 'the relation between national fitness and women's activities to their terrifying extreme.' Moreover, racial thinking remained basic to ideas about the accumulation of property. It was important, Liu concluded, to recognise that when historians are studying differences between men and women, and between women themselves, that 'we are in fact studying race as a principle of social organization and racial metaphors as part of the process of defining hierarchies and constituting boundaries of privilege'.

One of the first American historians to recognise the imperialist underpinnings of the writings of feminist historians was Antoinette Burton. Burton echoed Barkley Brown in regretting the fact that 'the historical relationship of feminism to European imperialist ideologies remains largely unexamined . . .'.[50] She pointed out that many British feminists in the late nineteenth century 'justified women's equality on the grounds that, as women, they contributed to the survival and the continued prosperity of the British Empire'. They did not regard Indian women as equals, but as their especial responsibility, their burden, and their belief in a 'global sisterhood' ignored the differences between British and Indian cultures. At the end of the article, she emphasised the importance of recognising that any feminist movement is a product of 'discrete historical circumstances', when she pointed out that late twentieth-century feminism was in part a product of those 'who saw the world in terms of colonial hierarchies and who envisioned something like a true "universal womanhood" in their own imperial self-image'. Burton has extended her study of the 'traces of empire' in British culture to how Indians who came to 'the so-called motherland' encountered 'English people and and prejudices on English soil'.[51]

Antoinette Burton's awareness of the imperialism of nineteenth-century feminism was part and parcel of her insistence that those who produced historical narratives of feminist movements be aware of the fact that those productions were themselves historical. She agreed with Liz Stanley and Mineke Bosch that those who wrote feminist histories should not to 'essentialize "feminism" by making it appear singular, static and unmediated either by its various historical contexts or by the historians who produce it'.[52] Similarly, she criticised those who used 'Western feminist experiences as their exclusive point of reference for "feminism" as historically considered, and those that fail to come to terms with the ethnocentric/imperial/ racist ideologies which structured the white middle-class feminist of Europe and America'. Burton contributed to a special issue of *Women's Studies International Forum* in 1990 which was concentrated on 'Western Women and Imperialism.'[53] There she asserted that the 'influence of imperial culture on feminist ideology should be no more surprising than, for example the impact of the industrial revolution on women's lives, or of liberal individualist discourse on the Victorian women's movement'. And it was, she pointed out, generally agreed among historians that 'a sense of national and racial superiority based on Britain's imperial status was an organizing principle of Victorian culture'. For Burton feminism is 'as much a quest for power as a battle of rights', and one way Victorian feminists sought for power was through 'allying their cause with British imperial rule'. They thus 'collaborated in the ideological work of empire' and left modern western feminism with a racist legacy.

Modern feminist historians clearly wished to take part in the struggle against racial and colonial oppression, or at least to become aware of the part played by women in the past in that oppression. The association of feminism with an ideology of liberation is implicit in the approach of those who saw themselves as feminist historians of women. Judith Butler pointed out that colonisation and oppression could arise through the exercise of power by historians themselves. She argued that the concept of patriarchy as a universal and transcultural abstraction could be used to override and suppress the particular characteristics of 'gender asymmetry'.[54] She stressed the particular importance of this struggle against what she termed a 'colonizing epistemological strategy' at a time when feminists were seeking to become involved in struggles against racial and colonial oppression. The controversy over the uses and abuses of the term 'patriarchy' emerged again in 1993. Judith Bennett understood this controversy as part of the continuing dialogue between those influenced by 'left and socialist ideologies in the development of feminism and women's history', and those like herself, who 'reflect radical feminist theories which . . . have focussed more exclusively on gender relations and women's oppression'.[55] Representing the first position was Bridget Hill, a historian of the eighteenth century. In an article in *Women's History Review*, Hill criticised in no uncertain terms the views of Judith Bennett as expressed in both the Review essay and the article on 'Feminism and History' which were considered in Chapter Five.[56] Bennett's 'proposed approach to women's history, and more particularly to the history of women's work' was, Hill, declared, 'both wrong and a-historical'. The crux of her disagreement with Bennett was that the latter had taken to extremes the thesis that the nature of women's work was unvarying. She accused Bennett of placing the study of patriarchy in a hierarchical position, an approach which, wrote Hill, was 'mistaken', and distorted the history of women. Morever, she argued, as 'a thesis that turns its back on many of the assumptions of social, labour and economic history it can only result in greater isolation' for women's historians. Concerned to carry men with women historians of women, she agreed that patriarchy must be kept 'firmly within our sights and theirs', but asserted that it could not be separated out from economic factors: 'what historians of women confront is a whole and not a segmented reality . . .'.

In her reply, Judith Bennett denied that she had argued that 'there has been no change in women's lives', but had 'instead suggested that the pace of change, the motors of change, and the realities of change differ for women and men'.[57] She also denied prioritising patriarchy and referred to her own advocacy of 'looking at how patriarchal structures have interacted with economic systems'.[58] She was curious about the intensity of Hill's reactions to 'the project of historicising patriarchy', and suggested that it was a concept which attracted 'so much fear and loathing that it cannot, for some people, be treated in a rational and moderate fashion'.[59] In Bennett's view, it was vitally important to study the workings of patriarchy in order to understand the subordination of women; a failure to do so would mean that 'the lives of both women and men will continue to be twisted by the per-verse power of patriarchal institutions.'[60] In the concluding chapter of her latest book, *Ale, Beer and Brewsters in England: Women's Work in a Changing World, 1300–1600,* Bennett argued that 'as we more fully appreciate differ-ences among women, we also must not forget differences between women and men'.[61] One of her conclusions from the period the book covered was that 'English patriarchy in these centuries was . . . particularly strong because it sprang from many sites, all of which, while buttressing patriarchy, also served other critical functions.'[62] She contended that her study had 'illuminated, for one historical setting, some critical aspects of patriarchal power: its multiplicity; its production as an effect of essential social institutions; its flexibility; its endurability . . .'.[63]

An emphasis on the complexity of the operations of patriarchy, and a critique of some of the broad generalisations made by historians of women was expressed in the work of Amanda Vickery, a historian of the eighteenth century. Vickery belongs to a new generation of historians whose roots do not lie in the women's movement. The argument of her historiographical review published in 1993 was that the two 'stories' told by historians of women focusing on two key periods – the early modern and the nineteenth century – the story of a 'golden age' for women when there was much greater equality between the sexes, and the story of the emergence of 'separ-ate spheres' which destroyed this co-operative project – were in conflict.[64] Pinning down the inherent contradictions, she wrote: 'The problem is ex-emplified if we try to reconcile Susan Amussen's work on early-modern Norfolk with Leonore Davidoff's on nineteenth-century Suffolk. Are we to believe that women were driven out of a public sphere of production and power in one district in the seventeenth century, while just over the county border the same development was delayed by well over a hundred years?' She concluded that the 'economic chronologies upon which the accounts of women's exclusion from work and their incarceration in domesticity depend are deeply flawed'. It was possible to see the 'marginalization of middle-class women' in any period you chose to look. She accepted that 'the notion of the separate spheres in particular has done modern women's history a great service' in moving it beyond 'a whiggish celebration of the rise of feminism, or a virtuous rediscovery of those previously hidden from history'.

The assertion that the ideology of separate spheres was instrumental in class formation made gender significant, but now, she asserted, 'new categories and concepts must be generated' in order to 'map the breadth and boundaries of female experience'. She called for a more rigorous analysis of printed sources: '"intertextuality" must be researched, not simply asserted in the abstract'. Case studies and long-range analyses of the debates on women's 'proper role' were needed in order to 'establish whether the rhetoric of domesticity and private spheres contributed to female containment, or instead was simply a defensive and impotent reaction to public freedom already won'.

In 1998 Vickery brought out a book in which she argued that there had been no retreat into domesticity among the gentry of Yorkshire in the period between 1750 and 1820.[65] Part of her argument was a challenge to the dominant idea that the 'eighteenth-century man-midwife or surgeon' was a villain the imposition of whose authority upon women represented a 'patriarchal victory'.[66] She also emphasised that, however stoical, the childbearing woman was not necessarily 'supine in the face of custom and authority'.[67] Vickery's women were no victims of patriarchal power: they made their own choices and played an active part in the public sphere. In the opinion of one of the book's reviewers 'what constituted "the public sphere" changed in eighteenth-century England'.[68] The question of what constituted 'the public', a concept interrogated by Joan Landes in 1988, was still crucial to studies of women, and, as the work of John Tosh, described Chapter Seven, demonstrates, to studies of men.

In the article summarised earlier, Mineke Bosch suggested that most feminist historians were excited by 'the gender debate'. However, Bosch herself 'often experienced difficulty in participating in the debate, not because of the abstract level or intricate argumentation, but because every historian adheres to her own vision, her own interpretation, related to her own feminist, intellectual, national and cultural background. Theory is as much influenced by local discursive relations as is every other text'.[69] Historians of women in the nineties were choosing separate, if often linked paths through the thicket of theoretical approaches. Those choices were shaped by their differing cultural heritages, political perspectives and by their friendship networks, but also by philosophical positions on ontological questions and these positions were perhaps more personal than cultural. Arguments about issues such as the possibility of recovering the experience of women in the past in ways which could be judged as better or more accurate were intensely argued but there was widespread agreement on the worthwhileness of continuing with the project of writing women into history. There was an increasing emphasis on the complexity and breadth of the process, and a continued exhilaration in participating. The uncertainty about 'what women's history should be' which was expressed at the eighth Berkshire Conference of Women's History did not mark any diminution in the productiveness of historians of women.[70]

Notes and references

1. Kali A.K. Israel, 'Writing inside the kaleidoscope: re-representing Victorian women public figures', *Gender & History*, 2:1 (Spring, 1990), pp. 40–8. Sheila Rowbotham, 'The trouble with patriarchy', in Raphael Samuel, ed., *People's History and Socialist History* (London, 1989), p. 365.

2. *Signs*, 15:4 (Summer, 1990), pp. 848–60. Linda Gordon, *Heroes of Their Own Lives: The Politics and History of Family Violence* (New York, 1988). Joan Wallach Scott, *Gender and the Politics of History* (New York, 1988).

3. Catherine Hall, 'Politics, poststructuralism and feminist history', *Gender & History*, 3:2 (Summer, 1991), pp. 204–10.

4. Liz Stanley, editorial introduction to 'British feminist histories', *Women's Studies International Forum*, 13: 1–2 (Spring and Summer, 1990), pp. 3–7.

5. Liz Stanley, 'Rescuing "women" in history from feminist deconstructionism', in ibid., pp. 151–7.

6. Karen Offen, Ruth Roach Pierson and Jane Rendall, eds., *Writing Women's History: International Perspectives* (Basingstoke, 1991).

7. Jane Rendall, 'Uneven developments', in ibid., p. 52.

8. Ibid., p. 50.

9. Ibid., p. 51.

10. Stanley (1990), p. 154.

11. Gisela Bock, 'Challenging dichotomies: developments in women's history', in Offen, Pearson and Rendal, eds. (1991), p. 6.

12. Ibid., p. 16.

13. Ibid., p. 17.

14. Mineke Bosch, 'The future of women's history', *Gender & History*, 3:2 (Summer, 1991), pp. 139–46.

15. Louise Newman, 'Dialogue: critical theory and the history of women: what's at stake in deconstructing women's history', *Journal of Women's History*, 2:3 (Winter, 1991), pp. 58–68.

16. Newman paraphrased a passage from Mary Poovey, *Uneven Developments* (London, 1989), p. 18.

17. Ruth Roach Pierson, 'Experience, difference, dominance and voice', in Offen, Pierson and Rendall, eds. (1991), p. 80.

18. Ibid.

19. Ibid., p. 94.

20. Ibid.

21. Judith Butler and Joan Wallach Scott, eds., *Feminists Theorize the Political* (London, 1992).

22. Ibid., p. 26.

23. Ibid., pp. 34, 37.

24. Ibid., p. 12.

25. Judith Butler, *Gender Trouble: Feminism and the Subversion of Identity* (New York and London, 1990).

26. Ibid., p. ix.

27. Butler and Scott, eds. (1992), p. 15.

28. Kathleen Canning, 'Dialogue: the turn to gender and the challenge of poststructuralism', *Journal of Women's History*, 5:1 (Spring, 1993), pp. 104–13.

29. Ute Schmidt, 'Problems of theory and method in feminist history' in Joanna de Groot and Mary Maynard, eds., *Women's Studies in the 1990s: Doing Things Differently* (Basingstoke, 1993).

30. Ibid., p. 88.

31. Ibid., p. 95.

32. Ibid., p. 96.

33. Ibid., p. 97.

34. Catherine Hall, *White, Male and Middle-Class: Explorations in Feminism and History* (Cambridge, 1992), p. 1.

35. Ibid., p. 24.

36. Ibid., p. 33.

37. Ibid., p. 34.

38. Ibid., p. 25.

39. Anna Davin, 'Imperialism and motherhood', *History Workshop Journal*, 5 (Spring, 1978), pp. 9–65.

40. Valerie Amos and Pratibha Parmar, 'Challenging imperial feminism', *Feminist Review*, 17 (Autumn, 1984), pp. 3–19.

41. Ibid., p. 3.

42. Elsa Barkley Brown, 'Polyrhythms and improvization: lessons for women's history', *History Workshop Journal*, 31 (Spring, 1991), pp. 85–91.

43. Evelyn Brooks Higginbotham, 'African-American women's history and the meta-language of race', *Signs*, 17:2 (Winter 1992), pp. 251–74.

44. Darlene Clark Hine, 'Black women's history, white women's history: the junction of race and class', *Journal of Women's History*, 4:2 (Autumn, 1992), pp. 125–33.

45. Ann Laura Stoler, 'Carnal knowledge and imperial power', in Joan Scott, ed., *Feminism & History* (Oxford, 1998), p. 210.

46. Ibid., p. 252.

47. Vron Ware, *Beyond the Pale* (London, 1992), p. xvi.

48. Ibid., p. 37.

49. Tessie Liu, 'Teaching the differences among women from a historical perspective', *Women's Studies International Forum*, 14:4 (Winter 1991), pp. 265–76.

50. Antoinette Burton, 'The feminist quest for identity: British imperial suffragists 1900–15', *Journal of Women's History*, 3: 2 (Summer, 1991), pp. 46–81.

51. Antoinette Burton, *At the Heart of the Empire: Indians and the Colonial Encounter in Late-Victorian Britain* (California, 1998), p. 3.

52. Antoinette Burton, ' "History" is now: feminist theory and the production of historical feminisms', *Women's History Review*, 1:1 (1992), pp. 25–38.

53. Antoinette Burton, 'The white woman's burden: British feminists and the Indian woman, 1865–1915', *Women's Studies International Forum*, 13:4 (Winter, 1990), pp. 293–308.

54. Butler (1990), p. 35.

55. Judith Bennett, 'Women's history: a study in continuity and change', *Women's History Review*, 2:2 (1993), pp. 173–85.

56. Bridget Hill, 'Women's history: a study in change, continuity or standing still?', *Women's History Review*, 2:1 (1993), pp. 5–22.

57. Bennett (1993), p. 176.

58. Ibid., p. 178.

59. Ibid., pp. 178–9.

60. Ibid., p. 179.

61. Judith Bennett, *Ale, Beer and Brewsters in England: Women's Work in a Changing World, 1300–1600* (Oxford, 1996), p. 153.

62. Ibid., p. 155.

63. Ibid., p. 154.

64. Amanda Vickery, 'Golden Age to Separate Spheres? A review of the categories and chronology of English women's history', *The Historical Journal*, 30:2 (1993), pp. 383–412.

65. Amanda Vickery, *The Gentleman's Daughter: Women's Lives in Georgian England* (New Haven, Conn., 1998).

66. Ibid., p. 94.

67. Ibid., p. 96.

68. Ruth Perry, 'Women and daughters', *History Workshop Journal*, 47 (Spring, 1999), pp. 292–6.

69. Bosch (1991), pp. 140–1.

70. *The Chronicle of Higher Education* (5 July 1990), p. A6.

CHAPTER SEVEN

The shape of an historical community
1993–9

The 1990s have been a period of abundant research and publication by historians of women. Merry Wiesner wrote in the introduction to a book published in 1998 that in 1974 it had been possible for her to read most of what had been written on women in the medieval and early modern period in Europe.[1] By the mid-nineties book-length studies numbered in the hundreds and articles in the thousands. The respectability of the enterprise of writing women into history is marked by such events as the launching in September 1998 of a three-year project financed by the Leverhulme Trust on the contribution of the Enlightenment to feminism. The project is directed by Barbara Taylor and is collaborative and comparative, involving seventy specialists. Historians of women are no longer restricted to the margins. The impact of women's history on the broader discipline may be exemplified by the work of a historian of a younger generation whose writing demonstrates the recognition of the significance of women in history although it does not have women as its main focus. Linda Colley's *Britons: Forging the Nation 1707–1837* was published in 1992 to great acclaim. Colley stated in a newspaper interview that she had never felt disadvantaged as a woman academic, and perhaps because her personal academic history had protected her from male prejudice until fairly late on in her career, she did not become a historian of women. This did not mean that she remained unaware of what she referred to as 'the residual sexism of British historiography'.[2] Women are firmly present in *Britons*: Colley records both their political involvement and the 'male anxieties about female pretensions' which 'became markedly sharper in the second half of the eighteenth century'.[3]

A variety of perspectives continues to characterise and to some extent still disturbs while it enlivens the writing of historians of women. Merry

Wiesner's view is that 'the study of early modern women and gender is almost over-theorized, with every theoretical school seeming to have something to offer'; listing post-colonialism, socialist feminism, poststructuralism, cultural materialism, psycholanalysis and the new historicism.[4] In this chapter one focus will be on the debates around the validity of poststructuralist ideas as historians of women sought positions which provided some stability. Fundamental was the issue of whether historians could claim to be searching after the truth in any meaningful way. A historian's judgement of the adequacy of the facts of history lay in their claim to be 'about something outside discourse'.[5] If it was accepted that they could not, then the political project of feminist history – what Linda Gordon had described as its 'mythic power' – was shaken. The claim that sources from the past were 'texts' and merely 'representations' which had no purchase on the reality to which they referred seemed to place the writing of historians about those texts in the same category as fiction. The response of some historians of women to these threats to the writing of the history of the experience of women as agents of history has been described in the preceding chapter: the threads of that narrative will be picked up again here. Concern about the continued control of the discipline of history by men was also expressed; sometimes in conjunction with concern about the encroachment of poststructuralist ideas. The penultimate section of this chapter offers an outline of the contours of the writing of the history of gender at the end of the century by looking at a variety of texts, including two personal reviews through their own writing of thirty years of 'gender and the historian' by Lee Davidoff and Gerda Lerner.

First, I want to look at a development which began before the nineties, the beginnings of a writing of the history of masculinity which Jane Rendall had identified as an essential task. Men had been the actors on the stage of history for a hundred years before the late 1960s: they were the invisible, unstudied norm against which women had implicitly been measured. Nathalie Zemon Davis had written as early as 1976 of the need to write the history of both women and men: 'we should not be working only on the subjected sex any more than an historian of class can focus exclusively on peasants.'[6] But the priority for women historians had been to write studies which focused primarily on women, so that the instability of the category men remained relatively neglected until the 1990s. In 1989 Gisela Bock identified the absence of histories which were specific to men: 'While the imperative that women's history always be related to men's has become commonplace, up to now the reverse has hardly been true.'[7] Men still appeared to exist beyond gender relations. A review essay by David Morgan in this same issue looked at books with historical perspectives, but he referred to them as belonging to 'Men's Studies', and their genesis is in sociology. The book under review which has the most specifically historical focus is a collection of essays which Morgan described as 'under-theorised'. In 1991 a collection of essays edited by John Tosh and Michael Roper, *Manful Assertions*, looked at constructions of masculinity in labour, business, religion, education and national identity in Britain over the past 200 years.[8] Tosh then went on to develop a thesis which asserted the significance of masculinity in the late nineteenth century in the linked arenas of work, home and all-male associations.[9] Masculinity was formed from a balance between these minimal components, a connection characterised by contradiction and instability. Tosh was convinced that these components are contingent and vulnerable rather than fixed outside the narrative of social change.

In 1999 Tosh published a study one of whose focal points was men's place in the private sphere: as he pointed out, men's place in the private sphere had not had a central place in the reclaiming of the private as a valid focus for historical study.[10] Another conceptual context to Tosh's study is the questioning of the validity of the distinction between the private and public spheres; he perceives much of men's power as residing 'in their privileged freedom to pass at will between the public and the private'.[11] An essential aspect of patriarchy was domestic: 'men have usually wielded authority within the home' and 'it has been necessary for their masculine self-respect that they do so'.[12] Men's relationship with the private and the domestic had been noted by Judith Newton as part of a warning concerning male appropriation of the feminine. She wrote in 1991: 'My own work on nineteenth-century culture suggests that male writers regularly appropriated domestic values in order to extend the authority of male social critique.'[13] In his book Tosh examined the preconditions of the establishment of British patriarchal domesticity and its climax in the mid-nineteenth century. He exposed its 'serious inner contradictions' which led to visible strain and then decline as home became increasingly associated with the feminine, and empire displaced domestic concerns at the end of the century.[14] Tosh's study is of middle-class men, and he had earlier acknowledged that working-class men's commitment to the home was even more problematic: masculinity had multiple social meanings in the nineteenth century.[15] But he was anxious to emphasise that 'gender status cannot be reduced to class status, citing Davidoff and Hall's *Family Fortunes* as a demonstration of the way a focus of gender does not simply 'fill out the gender attributes of a class we already know about', but places 'gender at the centre of class formation itself'.

Tosh's understanding of patriarchal forms are that they 'have arisen from psychic needs combined with a perception of the material advantage to be derived from power over women'.[16] In his 1994 article Tosh looked briefly at masculinity as 'a *subjective* identity', giving a glimpse of 'the quick-sand of psychoanalytical theory'. It was only a glimpse because of what he sees as the difficulty historians experience in finding appropriate sources. When discussing the aspect of masculine identity which depended on juxta-position to a demonised 'other', Tosh again cited Catherine Hall; this time for her more recent work on Empire. Hall has been examining the way English national identities and ideas about citizenship have been constructed through powerful notions of sexual and racial difference.[17] Historians of women were increasingly emphasising the fact that while femininity is certainly unstable and problematic, 'studies of masculinity suggest that discourses of masculinity are also fractured and insecure'.[18] The difficulties of writing about 'the transformation of men, concepts of masculinity and male identities' was explored by Paul Stigant, a literary scholar with a 'particular interest in the history of gender and forms of consciousness' in the introduction to a book on the involvement of men in the struggle for women's suffrage.[19] He noted that 'there is no accepted narrative or chro-nology of gender relations for twentieth-century Britain'. The absence of such a story made it difficult, Stigant suggested, to be certain 'what story or whose story this book is telling; or, perhaps more grandly, of what meta-narrative it is a part'.[20]

Historians in the eighties had been wary of meta-narratives. In the mid-nineties two ambitious projects provided the structure of a history of gender relations from the early modern period onwards. Olwen Hufton presented a narrative of early modern women in *The Prospect Before Her: A History of Women in Western Europe, 1500–1800*.[21] She declared that her book was 'about the interaction between beliefs about what was appropriate to men and women and what occurred in the practices of daily life'. This last phrase signalled her adherence to the idea that the historian could write about 'the wider social and economic framework, a specific material world' as something separate from 'ideas about gender' which, she wrote, 'were only one thread in an entire web of beliefs'.[22] Hufton's understanding of gender history is one 'in which the particular responses of each of the two sexes and the interaction between them is given weight . . .'.[23] She traced the move – strongly influenced by cultural history – towards what she sees as a focus on 'text, language and visual representations', and her reference there is to Scott.[24] Hufton believes this approach 'has been particularly revelatory when applied to micro-history, that is, the close examination of small incidents or case histories so as to give not merely a narrative account but an interpretation of events by using psychoanalysis, psychology, semi-otics and all the tools of social science'.[25] However, her view is that 'it has proved difficult to transfer this approach on to a broader canvas without straying into the realms of conjecture . . .'. Moreover, the result has carried the risk of erecting 'the theoretical or "generic" woman and man, versions of womanhood and manhood, at the expense of what was, as far as one can discern, the experience or real people'.[26] She added that 'in attempting to understand the significance of rituals and cultural rules, insufficient attention has been given to the material constraints which determined the lives of the vast majority of people'.[27] Her own book was clearly intended to offer both the attention to the material, and the sort of broader generalisations which she believed were valid.

The second, and much more large-scale project originated from a proposal made in 1987 by an Italian publisher to a group of French historians and came to fruition in the early nineties: a five-volume *History of Women in the West* from antiquity to the present.[28] In a brief prelude to the first volume, Joan Scott and Nathalie Zemon Davis explained that the intention was to provide food for the appetite of readers of the French and Italian public for 'books of high quality on history', and to counteract the neglect of the study of women and gender by the universities.[29] The overall editors were two French historians of women, Georges Duby and Michelle Perrot. In their introduction to the first volume, Duby and Perrot wrote that the questions it sought to answer were concerned with the operation and representation of the relations between the sexes. They accepted the view that men had dominated women 'throughout history', but saw this domination as varying widely, and it was this variation which was the object of study of the series.[30] Their history, they declared, 'is fundamentally relational; because we look at society as a whole, our history of women is necessarily also a history of men'. In an introduction to the third volume Duby and Perrot defined their outlook as 'feminist' in the sense that it was egalitarian.[31] This would not be a definition acceptable to all who call themselves feminist, but by focusing on 'women' in both the title of the series and the content of the articles contained within it, the authors perhaps offered a bridge between women's and gender history: theirs was a study of gender and of patriarchy.

Hufton had clarified some of the problems for historians of attempting to put Joan Scott's exhortations into practice while continuing with a more traditional way of writing history. A much angrier response to Scott's ideas appeared under the title 'Gender as Postmodern Category of Paralysis' in the *Women's History Review* in 1994.[32] It was written by Joan Hoff, a legal historian, and Professor at Bloomington, Indiana, who described herself as a 'stubborn relic from the 1960s and tenured guerrilla to boot'. The first of the three prongs of her attack on postmodernism was that it was 'ahistorical and misogynist, as well as politically paralyzing'. She alleged that poststructuralist theories had been devised by Foucault and other men 'whose theories were equally insensitive or hostile to half the human population', and whose 'male-defined definition of gender . . . erased woman as a category of analysis'. The adoption of them by historians of women was motivated by elitism, ethnocentrism and 'the impulse . . . to impose the fragmentation of the present on the past'. She also identified a 'generational conflict', suggesting that a younger generation of historians was motivated by a search for professional identity and career advancement in choosing a methodology and theory based on the rejection of the experiences, and memories of those experiences, of the 'pioneer generation of historians of women'. The ability of US historians to adopt new theories was a luxury, she asserted, that was not shared by women in 'most other countries' where there had been no such pioneer generation. The intellectual dangers to historians of 'postmodern theory', Hoff argued, were the hostility to linear time and to the operations of cause and effect, and the undermining of ideas about reality and truth. The analysis of representation, the 'linguistic turn', reduced 'the experiences of women, struggling to define themselves and better their lives in particular historical contexts, to mere subject stories'. 'Flesh and blood women' became social constructs and 'material experiences become abstract representations'. The changing of the concept of gender from 'the material and cultural representation of sex' to a 'totally abstract representation of sexual and other kinds of differences' had destroyed 'any collective concept of woman or women through the fragmentation of the female subject'. The political damage of this change was the undermining and thus the depoliticisation of gender, and the removal of meaning from feminist politics, just when 'women and minorities were beginning to find their voices and speak out with a collective identity'.

The reply in *Women's History Review* to this attack did not appear for another two years. June Purvis, the editor of the journal, received a variety of responses to the article, including one which suggested that she should not have published it. Purvis pointed out that *Women's History Review* was intended to be a forum for debate, and in the first issue in 1996, a response by Susan Kingsley Kent and a reply to that response by Joan Hoff was published.[33] Kent was the author of *Sex and Suffrage*, described in Chapter Four, and of *Making Peace: The Reconstruction of Gender in Interwar Britain*. In her introduction to the latter book Kent had acknowledged her debt to 'poststructuralist theories of language' and in particular, to the work of Denise Riley.[34] Kent was clearly angered by Hoff's article, and decided that 'the vitriol with which Hoff addresses those engaged in gender history cannot go unremarked'. She responded by accusing Hoff of patronising historians from other countries, and of attempting 'to silence or cow the individuals whose work she so disdains'. She suggested that Hoff's 'anxiety' might be 'misplaced rage and fear' which arose from 'the nostalgic desire for a return to a unified female subjectivity that would obviate both the need to acknowledge conflicts between women and an analysis of the power relations that render white women complicit in the oppression of women of colour'. In Kent's view, Hoff failed to recognise the need to critique the political origins of the concept of a stable identity for women which had privileged white middle-class women. Catherine Hall had claimed that women of colour were the originators of the challenge to the dominance implicit in such privileging: Kent acknowledged their role and juxtaposed it with the contribution of poststructuralists. Far from abandoning politics, history and women, historians 'who use the tools of deconstruction to write about gender' were seeking – and here she quoted Joan Scott – ' "to understand the operations of the complex and changing discursive processes by which identities are ascribed, resisted or embraced" '.

It was precisely phrases such as these which discomfited some historians. In a brief contribution to the debate, Carol Ramazanoglu, a sociologist, challenged in moderate and clear terms the exclusive focus of poststructuralists on 'questions of *how* we know what we know', because it had displaced 'questions of *what* needs to be known and *why*'.[35] She agreed that it was indeed useful to question 'why we think as we do, and how else we might think about the nature and effects of power', but she added that if 'we want to understand embodied lives and how and *why* gender relations have been and are *lived*', then it was necessary to continue to struggle with the task of 'justifying ways of taking accounts of experience as sources of knowledge'. Hoff's own 'Reply to my Critics' repeated Ramazanoglu's understanding of history's concern with '*what* needs to be known and *why*' as a corrective to the 'disembodied discourses' of poststructuralism.[36] Hoff expressed her belief that 'Scott has yet to produce a researched scholarly work based on her own original or modified poststructuralist theories'. For her, the 'expectations about the empowerment of diversity' which poststructuralists raised were exaggerated and led to false hope. The first part of her 'Reply' consisted in a riposte to Kent's accusation that she had not read Foucault. She accused Kent of ignoring Foucault's *Archaeology of Knowledge* in which he developed the notion of the archive in order to 'retain the non-discursive as a separate analytic field'. The possibility of using Foucault's ideas without losing touch with the material was to be a recurrent theme in the reactions of other historians of women to poststructuralist ideas in the nineties.

An article with the title 'Beyond the "Big Three": the development of feminist theory into the 1990s' in *Women's History Review* in the autumn of 1995 overtly called for a halt to the flight from the material, but argued that it was possible to make use of poststructuralist ideas without losing touch with the political weapons necessary to feminism.[37] The author was a philosopher, Mary Maynard. The 'changing emphases' in feminist thought which she identified are indeed those which have appeared on the pages of this book: the shift to textual analysis under the impetus of poststructuralist

arguments; the fragmenting of identity which appeared to render experience obsolete; the criticism of meta-narratives, in particular those which
imply a vision of history as linear and progressive; the abandonment of
monocausal explanations and monolithic understandings of the operation
of power, and the hegemonic emphasis on culture. Maynard argued that
some of the effects of such changes threatened to remove the ground from
underneath feminist thought. Her view is that feminist ideas depend both
on categories such as women and gender which were in danger of being
deconstructed out of existence, and on a 'reality' which is outside of language. But she saw possible ways of avoiding the pitfalls while retaining the
insights of 'Lacanian and post-structuralist perspectives'. She claimed that
whereas the idea of a unified self might well be false, this did not mean that
'it comprises nothing but persistent and ephemeral fluctuations'. Citing
Jane Flax's argument that there is a useful distinction to be made between
the 'unitary' self and the 'core' self, Maynard concluded that there was no
need to 'abandon the notion of the subject altogether'; such a conclusion
meant that it was possible to retain the connected idea of agency. On
the question of metanarratives Maynard's view was that those based on
'universalisations' were clearly unacceptable, but that this did not mean
that it was impossible to generalise, if such an activity is understood as
partial and provisional. As for the concept 'woman', she made a distinction
between its use as a the unitary category which needed to be avoided, and
its use as a '*unifying* term . . . around which a sense of commonality and
community might be developed'. Moving on the complex question of
materiality, Maynard asserted that 'our lived experience is mediated not
just through discourse or text but through material structures and relationships also', and she denied that 'events, relations and social formations do
not have conditions of existence and real effects outside the sphere of the
discursive . . .'.

Mary Maynard's assertion of the possibility of retaining concepts of
experience, subjectivity and identity which were central to the writing of
history had been cogently made the previous year in an article by Kathleen
Canning; 'Feminist history after the linguistic turn'.[38] Canning defined 'the
linguistic turn' as 'a catch-all phrase for divergent critiques of established
historical paradigms, narratives, and chronologies, encompassing not only
poststructuralist literary criticism, linguistic theory, and philosophy but also
cultural and symbolic anthropology, new historicism and gender history'.
She agreed with those who claimed that women's historians had provided
the first stepping-stones towards the linguistic turn, now the subject of intense disagreement among current practitioners. For social historians, she
reckoned, the most controversial aspect of the linguistic turn was precisely
the 'pivotal place' occupied by language which was seen not to reflect

reality but to 'constitute historical events and human consciousness'. As a 'historian of women who came of age during this sea change', Canning observed three reactions among feminists to it: resistance, welcome and 'strategic engagement'. Her own 'starting point' is that there is 'no turning back to the unreflective use of concepts such as experience or class', and in the article she offered a rewriting of the concepts of experience and discourse. While agreeing that it is difficult to separate language and experience, Canning is less happy with the 'one-dimensional notion that language or discourses "position subjects and *produce* their experiences"'. She found Scott's redefining of experience sometimes circular and her use of concepts of language, discourse and experience 'difficult to disentangle'. Noting the scepticism that Scott has at times expressed about the use of the concepts of resistance and agency, Canning was concerned that discourses themselves could only figure as 'fixed hegemonic systems without the intervention of agents . . .'. In a critique of an essay by Joan Scott on 'Women workers in the discourse of french political economy', Canning suggested that Scott had failed to place her analysis within the context of nineteenth-century French history, and had also omitted a consideration of what the outcome was of 'this discursive explosion'. Canning then offered an understanding of discourse which she described as 'a modified Foucauldian one of a convergence of statements, texts, signs, and practices across different, even dispersed sites (from courtrooms to street corners, for example) Implicit in the term *discourse*, as both a textual and social relation, is a certain expertise, the power and authority to speak, and the existence of a public sphere that transcends local settings'. Canning demonstrated her use of such a definition in an examination of a period in German history, the 1920s, when women workers succeeded in 'contesting the terms of the discourses that defined them'. In this example she traced the 'emergence of a counter discourse about the female body' which challenged both the 'seemingly disembodied (male) discourse of class politics and the colonizing claims of natalist reproductive politics on female bodies'. Like Lyndal Roper, whose approach to a different period of history is described below, Canning suggested that this example demonstrated that 'the body . . . offers an interesting and intricate way of retheorizing agency'.

Maynard had backed up her re-insertion of the material and the body into the history of women with the comment: 'Not everything is sign or text, as any rape survivor, homeless person or starving child will testify.'[39] She might have added Holocaust victim. In her introduction to a collection of essays, *Gender and Catastrophe*, Ronit Lentin was insistent that 'women know full well the meaning of "things" in their lives. "Things" such as genocide, hunger, displacement, sexual exploitation, war and migration cannot be dismissed as mere "words" or "accounts" as certain postmodernists would have us believe'.[40] She argued that 'genocides, wars, famines, slavery, the Shoah, ethnic cleansing and projects of mass rape and population control . . . must be gendered well beyond the discursive level'.[41] The worst catastrophes of history have tended to be analysed in terms which ignore gender: one essay in this volume rejected the assumption that gender was irrelevant to the Holocaust: 'For Jewish women the Holocaust produced a set of experiences, responses, and memories that do not always parallel those of Jewish men.'[42] Specifically, Jewish women were raped, became pregnant, had abortions, bore children and killed newborn babies. This list of horrors all concerned the body. For some historians who were quite prepared to allow the cogency of poststructuralism, the body was a point at which they challenged the validity of language as the sole medium of historical knowledge. Sally Alexander, for example, has found that 'the tension between the trials of subjectivity and historical agency . . . cannot be adequately grasped by the concept of an endless destabilization of language. Sexual difference is mediated by the body as well as phantasy . . .'.[43]

In an introduction to *Oedipus and the Devil: Witchcraft, Sexuality and Religion in Early Modern Europe*, Lyndal Roper wrote that the essays in the volume marked 'a shift on my part away from the conviction that gender is a product of cultural and linguistic practice, towards a view that sexual difference has its own physiological and psychological reality'.[44] Roper's *Holy Household*, published in 1989, had argued that gender relations 'far from being tangentially affected by the Reformation, were at the crux of the Reformation itself.'[45] Her later project, of which the essays represented 'a journey, not an arrival', was 'a history of early modern culture which will incorporate the subjective, the psychic and the corporeal . . .'.[46] The use of gender as a category of analysis had been, she acknowledged, 'immensely liberating'.[47] Gender as a concept had 'seemed to offer a way of giving feminists access both to anthropological history and discourse history', and deconstruction, with its assertion that sexual difference was the result of discourse, gave delight to the intellect.[48] But the way gender itself effects historical change remained vague. 'In the final analysis, gender, for all its splendid play of discursive variegation, remains a category whose content proves elusive, and whose causal claims are a cypher.'[49] She had 'come to think, along with other feminists writing now, . . . that feminist history, as I and others used to practise it, rested on a denial of the body'.[50] Looking at Judith Butler's rejection in *Gender Trouble* of the distinction between sex and gender, Roper detects there an implicit historical 'before' and 'after' in her argument which creates a different sort of binary distinction. Butler had, like others, 'sought to escape femininity by a flight from the body and a retreat to the rational reaches of discourse'.[51] Roper had come to the view that sexual difference had 'a bodily dimension' and sexual identity could 'never be satisfactorily understood if we conceive it as a set of discourses about masculinity and femininity'. What was needed was 'a history that can problematize the relation between the physical and the psychic'.[52] Roper's introduction offered a series of challenges to the direction in which historians were moving, one of which was 'to argue against an excessive emphasis on the cultural creation of subjectivity', and to pay attention to the psychic dimension of cultural practices – in particular, witchcraft.[53] She is concerned, perhaps most crucially, by the absence of any theory which satisfactorily linked individual subjectivity to cultural and social change: '. . . as historians, we often write as if social change impinges directly and uniformly upon the individual's mental structure, as if the psyche were a kind of blank sheet for social processes to write upon'.[54]

A comparison between Roper's volume of essays and a collection of essays edited by Joan Scott which appeared in 1996 gives a sense of the diversity and richness of both content and approach offered by historians of women in the 1990s. Roper's essays provided a vivid account, as she put it, of the 'preoccupations . . . of a very particular moment in the history of feminism when we have had to part with some illusions about what can be made anew'.[55] The essays in *Feminism & History* provided a review of the development of writing over a period.[56] The volume included several key articles published earlier in the nineties and already referred to in this book. Scott described them as addressing 'the question of identity as a problem of discourse or ideology in historical context'. Defining ideology as 'the organizing principle of social identity', she wrote that some historians preferred the term 'discourse to refer to the processes by which the facts of social difference are produced. Whatever the term, the goal is the same: to understand how social relationships are conceptualized and organized'.[57] In her introduction she presented a critique of the political grounds for the writing of feminist history. She opens with the comment that there has been 'a long history of feminists who write the history of women in order to make an argument for the equal treatment of women and men'.[58] She does not provide any personal comment on this approach, but implicit in her argument and quite explicit in her final paragraph is the view that the aims of feminism are much less straightforward than equality: for her feminism is a 'site where differences conflict and coalesce, where common interests are articulated and contested, where identities achieve temporary stability – where politics and history are made'.[59] One consequence of a political project where 'feminist history serves the political ends of feminism' was a contribution to an 'essentialized common identity of women'.[60] So, using women in history to 'legitimize feminist claims' involved treating women ahistorically: she accused – unnamed – historians of assuming that women in the past were fundamentally 'just like us'. Scott moved on to the now familiar territory of the way the analysis of the historical conditions which 'produced a shared identity of women' had revealed the differences between women's experiences and the influences which moulded them. The resulting tension between the idea of 'women' 'as a social category that pre-exists history' and the realisation of the immense variations in the 'social category of women' was difficult to live with, Scott recognised, yet 'is one of the most useful and productive tensions'.[61] She identified her own position within this tension, claiming that women do not 'exist as identical natural beings' outside of the political process which identifies them.[62] It is clear that her own preference is against 'describing difference' as a social fact, and in favour of 'analysing the history by which those differences have been produced', so that instead of 'enduring facts' they are 'the effects of contingent and contested processes of change'. Difference is then understood 'relative to specific contexts – to history'. Thus a woman's whiteness or Englishness was established in contrast to being black or being Indian: 'Identity did not inhere in one's body or nationality, but was produced discursively by contrasts with others.'[63]

In his review of the book, Kevin Passmore identified two kinds of essays within it; one group of authors were limited by a Derridean view to the task of 'uncovering the ways in which the discourses of the powerful position women as subjects'.[64] There was not much room for agency in these essays. Other authors, making use of the ideas of Foucault rather than Derrida, conceived of groups and individuals as able 'to formulate and pursue their own agendas, partly outside the reach of the powerful'. This distinction is also made in a review essay by Lyn Hunt. She refers to the argument put forward by Bunzl that 'Foucault's own historical analysis does not require' an anti-realist view of history.[65] In Hunt's view, a thorough Derridean deconstructive approach where all concepts are unstable is inherently contradictory, making it impossible, specifically, for Joan Scott 'to define any of her own concepts, such as gender, as the basis for concrete empiricist work . . .'.

In order to give a sense of the variety of forms of writing about women in history in the late nineties, I want to conclude with an outline of five pieces of writing published in 1997 and 1998: an article specifically concerned with theoretical approaches; a collection of essays on imperialism; a study of women in the second world war and finally two books of collected essays by two historians of women who have been working throughout the period of this book. The article, published in 1997, was written by Michele Riot-Sarcey.[66] She maintained that in France 'the bastions of political history have scarcely been challenged'. She began the article with a reference back to the declaration made by Michelle Perrot ten years earlier that women's history was only possible if 'the direction of the historical gaze' could be changed 'by making the question of relations between the sexes central'. Riot-Sarcey could detect scarcely any change in 'the direction of the historical gaze' in the preceding ten years: in her view the 'bastions of the discipline' in France, at least, remained 'firmly attached to the de facto legitimacy of masculine interpretations'. Referring to the epistemological discussions mainly conducted by Anglo-American historians, Riot-Sarcey agreed that it was time to 'put an end to the "discourse of truth" . . . so often reproduced as a universal model'. But she found that although 'the history of representations of women is attentive to cultural, mental and even unconscious constructions, the political dimension, fundamental in my eyes, is lacking'. Here there are echoes of the uneasiness of the French authors of 'Women's culture and women's power' discussed in Chapter Four. Riot's view is that discourse analysis cannot account for 'conflictual reality.' Not just in France, but in the US, the 'task of questioning the status of political history has only partially been undertaken'. The use of the category gender had 'shed light on the ways women have been excluded', but the process of exclusion was not, she argued 'merely the result of discourse' but was 'the consequence of specific practices central to the creation of social identities which shape given groups in their historical construction'. Although she made reference to the work of Joan Landes, described in Chapter Five, Riot-Sarcey's view was that political history still tended to be the 'triumphant narrative' of the victor. Even women who made subversive demands did so within the dominant discourse, simply in order to be heard. To reconstruct history was problematic precisely because of the process of domination contained within such conformity. So history itself must be taken as 'inherently problematic', and the historian must 'adopt a mode of enquiry aiming to track down the presuppositions behind utterance and the unthought lying behind practice in order to reveal as best we can the dynamic of power relations'.

Gender and Imperialism is a collection of essays, edited by Claire Midgeley.[67] The aim of the collection was to continue the by now well-sanctioned project of ensuring that histories of imperialism treat 'both coloniser and colonised . . . as gendered subjects, and that attention is paid to the ways in which imperial involvements and interactions were shaped by gender as well as race and class'.[68] In her introduction Midgeley accepted that writings about those who had been colonised was one form of the exercise of imperial power, and thus that the writing of imperial histories 'was – and to some extent remains – a key form of imperial discourse'.[69] One of the contributors to Midgeley's collection accepted that the historian cannot 'discern a real history beyond the limits of textual evidence', nor provide an 'authentic reconstruction' of the past.[70] Jane Haggis has found that Hayden White's depiction of history as fiction and narrative facilitated her writing, but she points out, citing Edward Said, that no historical text is disembodied. The idea that texts are 'worldly' and to some degree themselves 'events', limits the historian's choice of 'emplotment'.[71] The historian, unlike the fiction writer, is constrained by context. Midgeley, on the other hand, denied that history was 'no more than one form of fictional discourse', and rejected the slide which she observes from a critique of Imperial History which recognised it as a form of imperial discourse into 'hostility to the project of history writing as a whole'.[72] She retains a faith in 'the basic procedures of sound scholarship' and recommends the notion of a qualified objectivity as defined by the authors of *Telling the Truth about History.*[73] There Joyce Appleby, Lyn Hunt and Margaret Jacob had pointed out that the fact that 'narratives are human creations does not make them all equally fictitious or mythical . . . Postmodernism is itself a meta-narrative'.[74] While accepting the postmodernist identification of the impossibility of '"knowing the past completely"' they posited a 'qualified objectivity'; the result of an 'interactive relationship between an inquiring subject and an external object'.[75]

In her introduction to *Reconstructing Women's Wartime Lives* Penny Summerfield tackles directly the impact of postmodernism, citing in particular the writings of Denise Riley and Joan Scott. Summerfield writes that their approach 'deeply upset the world of women's history' because they seemed to constitute 'a recipe for abandoning the focus on women, individually and collectively . . .'.[76] Although she feels that this opposition to the poststructuralist position is understandable, she also hopes that it may have 'more to offer those seeking to use personal testimony as a historical source than appears at first sight'. She accepts dependence 'upon language for understanding who we are and what we are doing', and that the 'the meanings within language are cultural constructions collectively generated, historical deposits within the way we think, which constitute the framework within which we act'. But she quotes Judith Butler's view that 'construction is not opposed to agency; it is the necessary scene of agency . . .'. Granted that 'accounts of lived experience . . . should not be considered outside the discursive constructions' within which they were related, Summerfield yet sees some 'theoretical space for the study of the relationship between cultural constructions and consciousness, which would throw considerable light upon them both'.[77] She recalls the story Denise Riley told about her attempt to find out '"why and how people produce particular formulations about what they want"', and her verdict in the end that this was an impossible task. This conclusion led Riley to the theoretical position so inimical to Hoff's historical project. Riley had written that '"the attempt to lay bare the red heart of truth beneath the discolourations and encrustations"' assumed '"a clear space out of which voices can speak . . ."'.[78] Summerfield, on the other hand, suggested that the 'layers of meaning can become part of the subject of study', and quoted Kathleen Canning's intent to explore ' "the ways in which subjects mediated or transformed discourses in specific historical settings" '.[79] The subject and what she has to say about her experience is thus for Summerfield still worthy of study, even if 'the truth' about her experience cannot be ultimately laid bare. What she does in her book is analyse and interpret the voices expressed in oral testimony of women who remembered the Second World War, alongside the voices which spoke to those women. She accepted that 'the public framing of the meaning of experience (the creation of general or public discourse), takes place within male norms of action and control . . . which locate women within a particularly disadvantaged subject position', but argued that there existed 'multiple discourses concerning women's wartime lives'. Oral history offered a particular opportunity to explore the ways in which these discourses were ' "taken up" by women recounting their experiences'.[80]

Scott's *Feminism and History* looks back on the development of a period of writing the history of women: other historians did the same thing in a more personal manner. Carroll Smith-Rosenberg produced a collection of her own essays as early as 1985; the same project was completed by Catherine Hall in 1992, Sally Alexander in 1994 and Merry Wiesner in 1998. I will look at two other volumes here, one by a British and one by an American historian of women. Leonore Davidoff's collection of essays was published in 1995 under the title *Worlds Between*.[81] The essays had originally been published between the years 1974 and 1990, and they were written, Davidoff declared in her introduction, 'from the margins'. Their content and their conceptual approach arose from those concerns of society – housekeeping, domestic servants, landladies and lodgers, farmers' wives and daughters – 'seen as peripheral to historical and sociological interests'. But, as Davidoff swiftly pointed out, 'every centre must be defined by its rim', and a 'satisfying social analysis must take on the whole circumference'.[82] Davidoff had moved from studying the sociology of married women's work in the 1950s to a consideration of the historical dimensions of that question which was informed by her own experience of the division of labour while bringing up her children. Returning to academic work her changing perspective was 'fuelled' by her engagement with feminist thinking in the 1970s and 1980s, an analysis which 'uncovered . . . the hitherto unacknowledged gendered nature of institutions'.[83] The explanation for the extraordinary, but also complex, 'dominance of gendered categories' lay at least in part in power relations. One of the intentions of the essays included in *Worlds Between* was 'to expose the agency given to those in power'.[84] The final chapter seeks to come to grips with the 'postmodernist and deconstructionist ideas,' which 'had begun to tug at the edges of even the most basic traditional conceptual boundaries'. Davidoff accepted that as a result the 'exclusion of certain voices' had been exposed, and 'that it is *classification systems themselves* which determine what will be understood as "significant relationships"'. The direction in which such thinking took her was 'to go behind as well as beyond' the accepted models of work and home, abstract and embodied, masculine and feminine.[85] In a final optimistic paragraph to the introduction, Davidoff identified the 'ultimate aim of social analysis' was 'that all people might become aware of historical structures and of their own place within them'. Such recognition, she hoped, 'might possibly lead to sorely needed visions of renewal and reconstruction'.[86]

Gerda Lerner's *Why History Matters* appeared in 1997 and contained many of her published essays framed within an autobiographical introduction and a defence of history from which the book took its title.[87] Lerner's theoretical position implicit in these chapters remains staunchly realist and political. For her, history consists in the telling of stories, stories which extend 'human life beyond its span' and 'can give meaning to each life and serve as a necessary anchor for us'.[88] Because human beings need the personal and collective strength which comes through knowing their history, women have in the past been diminished by their absence from history. Human beings with a history can 'grow out of magical and mythical thought into the realm of rational abstraction', and 'make projections into the future that are responsible and realistic'.[89] The histories which Lerner implicitly approves are those which are 'balanced, complex and sophisticated versions of stories of the past', and those which threaten 'the hegemony of the history of the powerful'.[90] Women's history has restored the balance by challenging the 'selective memory' of 'the men who recorded and interpreted human history'. She accepts that '[H]istorical events are infinitely variable and their interpretations are a constantly shifting process. There are no certainties to be found in the past.'[91] Yet their discovering history has allowed women to 'learn their connectedness to the past' and the result has been the dramatic transformation of their consciousness.[92] Lerner's story is a personal one, involving 'group work, sharing of knowledge and sources, and at times, collective research and writing, and it has brought her a 'sisterhood . . . a meaningful intellectual and spiritual community'.[93] For Lerner, the writing of history was rooted in her feminist consciousness and her continuing challenge to patriarchy: 'We have not, as yet, created the new conceptual framework for the history of women, which will be created. These essays represent my contribution to that effort. They are my working tools and sign posts I have set up along the way on a road of discovery, which is leading both into the past and into the future.'[94]

* * * * * *

The main focus of this book has been on the way 'historians have con-ceptualized the body of historical knowledge . . .'.[95] There is a wealth of writing available on such thinking, since, as Joan Scott pointed out, 'His-torians of women have long been conscious of the need to articulate their relationship to History.'[96] Nathalie Zemon Davis examined the work of a small number of historians from the seventeenth and the first half of the twentieth centuries in order to assess how they 'placed their own life's work' within the body of knowledge which they assembled. Describing a portrait of the eighteenth-century historian Catherine Macaulay as both Clio and Liberty, Davis maintained that the elisions contained in such a three-fold representation 'have a double potentiality. On the one hand, they can obscure the tension between the living historian and the eternal body of history, making her prophetic or indignant rather than self-correcting. On the other, they can internalize that tension in a creative way, reminding the historian of a transcendent task and personal responsibility'.[97] This book is primarily concerned with the way historians of women understood their task and their responsibility. Zemon Davis's view is that 'when we debate what the subjects and methods of history should be, we are usually debating at the same time what the shape of the historical community should be and where we stand in it . . .'.[98] In the preceding chapters I have described a particular historical community and the debates within it about the subjects and methods which should be adopted.

The period under study – 1969–99 – is one where, to quote Joan Scott yet again, and for the final time, a 'profusion of histories has created a sense of fragmentation and confusion, characteristic perhaps of moments of pro-found intellectual transition'.[99] A diversity of approaches to the history of women was apparent from the start of this period. But it was also the case that there was a strong feeling of a community of historians of women, of a sisterhood and in the early years this was a group which was determinedly inclusive. Much of the drive for work on women received its impetus at first from the glaring absence of women from traditional history writing. Ex-planations for that absence were most obviously accessible in narratives of oppression, and the impetus for the liberation of women both in the past and in the present came from current feminist practice. Explanations for oppression were sought and found in the concept of patriarchy, and the nature and validity of this term were debated throughout the period cov-ered by this book. Accounts of oppression became increasingly complex over the ensuing years. The vital question which arose early on and was to be the crux of much deliberation was that of women's agency. There were two rather different issues at stake. One was the question of the paths taken by women towards their own liberation. Research which used sources writ-ten by women in the nineteenth century had led to a strong focus on

women's relationships with other women, a sisterhood of a previous generation. Debates centred on whether such a women's culture was a source of
feminism, or a culture which accepted the patriarchal understanding of
women's exclusive association with the private. The question of when and
whether women became associated with the private sphere was linked to
this debate. Later, agency was central to debates about appropriate theoretical
formations for understanding the past.

The history of writing the history of women is threaded through in this
period with politics. One of the drives to write such history was a feminist
impulse. Some historians of women happily accepted that their work was
motivated by their feminism; others were made uneasy by the possibility
that present-day concerns might distort understanding of the past. The
sense that the writing of history was an important weapon in the fight
against male domination lies behind some of the concerns expressed by
historians who were wary of working on women's culture, and behind the
caution and sometimes alarm of those who were defiant or circumspect in
their response to the ideas of Michel Foucault, Jacques Derrida and of
literary critics; ideas which are often placed under the umbrella title of
poststructuralist. From the first some feminist historians also engaged with
psychoanalytical thinking in the construction of their approach to the
writing of history.

The debates about the nature of the historical enterprise, given the power
of poststructuralist ideas to undermine the confident assertion that historians
could provide legitimate knowledge about the past, have taken a good deal
of space in the later chapters of this book. Historians of women had from
the first been critical of history as it had been written, so they were in the
forefront of the enterprise of examining the premises of traditional writing.
One of the attractions of gender as a concept was the understanding it
contained that sexual difference was historical, and therefore that it could
be changed. Subsequently some saw the tools of deconstruction and the concept of discourse as well-honed to transform the enterprise of history in ways
which could make a much bigger space available to women in history. Others
sensed that the result of the use of these tools was to disconnect history from
real bodies and real events and to make it an intellectual game. It is also
important to remember that the writing of history which was taking place
in parallel to these debates was often untouched by the ideas of poststructuralism. Many historians of women grappled with such ideas without alarm
and with varying degrees of delight, describing their positions in articles
and in the introductions to books. Faith in the ability of historical writing to
bring the reader in touch with the experience of real people in the past
through the careful and thorough scrutiny of source material, a deep at-
tachment to the archives and to the traditional methods of history endured.

In his review of *Feminism and History*, Kevin Passmore wrote: 'Whether gender theory will advance the cause of feminism is, in the end, rather difficult to say. There can, however, be little doubt of its contribution to the writing of history. The articles and chapters in *Feminism and History* represent some of the finest examples of modern historical scholarship. They demonstrate that gender studies have become the leading edge of academic history. It is the site not only of brilliant empirical work, but of the most advanced reflection on the nature of history as a discipline.'[100] Women are clearly visible in the landscape of history at the end of the century and gender studies rooted in history are myriad. The political project of feminist history is perhaps less secure precisely because of its political nature. The title of this book and of a recently published collection of essays which cover the same ground, *Gender and History in Western Europe*, are witness to both the tentative beginnings of some attention to masculinity, and an uneasiness about the terms 'women' and 'feminism'. Feminism has been inextricably implicated in the retrieval of women in history and in the emergence of gender studies. This book is a contribution to that project.

Notes and references

1. Merry Wiesner, *Gender, Church and State in Early Modern Germany* (London and New York, 1998), p. 1.

2. Linda Colley, *Britons: Forging the Nation 1707–1837* (London, 1992), p. 242.

3. Ibid., p. 239.

4. Wiesner (1998), pp. 1–2.

5. Sue Clegg, 'The feminist challenge to socialist history', *Women's History Review*, 6:2 (1997), pp. 201–13.

6. Nathalie Zemon Davis, ' "Women's History" in transition: the European case', *Feminist Studies*, 3:3/4 (Spring/Summer, 1976), p. 88.

7. Gisela Bock, 'Women's history and gender history: aspects of an international debate', *Gender & History*, 1:1 (Spring, 1989), p. 17.

8. John Tosh and Michael Roper, eds., *Manful Assertions: Masculinities in Britain since 1800* (London, 1991).

9. John Tosh, 'The making of masculinities: the middle-class in late nineteenth-century Britain', in Angela V. John and Claire Eustance, eds., *The Men's Share? Masculinities, Male Support and Women's Suffrage in Britain, 1890–1920* (London and New York, 1997).

10. John Tosh, *A Man's Place: Masculinity and the Middle-Class Home in Victorian England* (New Haven, Conn., 1999).

11. Ibid., p. 2.

12. Ibid., p. 3.

13. Judith Newton, 'Dialogue', *Journal of Women's History*, 2:3 (Winter, 1991), p. 104.

14. Tosh (1999), p. 7.

15. John Tosh, 'What should historians do with masculinity?', *History Workshop Journal*, 38 (Autumn, 1994), pp. 179–202.

16. Tosh (1994), p. 81.

17. Catherine Hall, 'Going a-Trolloping: imperial man travels the Empire', in Clare Midgeley, ed., *Gender and Imperialism* (Manchester, 1997).

18. Penny Summerfield, *Reconstructing Women's Wartime Lives* (Manchester and New York, 1998), p. 13.

19. John and Eustance, eds. (1997), pp. xviii, xi.

20. Ibid.

21. Olwen Hufton, *The Prospect Before Her: A History of Women in Western Europe, 1500–1800* (London, 1995).

22. Ibid., p. 5.

23. Ibid., p. 3.

24. Ibid., p. 4.

25. Ibid., p. 4.

26. Ibid., pp. 4–5.

27. Ibid., p. 5.

28. Georges Duby and Michelle Perrot, eds., *A History of Women in the West* (Cambridge, Mass., 1992–4)

29. Ibid., Vol. I, p. v.

30. Ibid., Vol. I, p. xx.

31. Ibid., Vol. III, p. ix.

32. Joan Hoff, 'Gender as a postmodern category of paralysis', *Women's History Review*, 3:2 (1994), pp. 149–68.

33. Susan Kingsley Kent, 'Mistrials and distribulations: a reply to Joan Hoff', *Women's History Review*, 5:1 (1996), pp. 9–18.

34. Susan Kinglsey Kent, *Sex and Suffrage in Britain, 1860–1914* (New Jersey, 1987); *Making Peace: The Reconstruction of Gender in Interwar Britain* (New Jersey, 1993).

35. Caroline Ramazanoglu, 'Unravelling postmodern paralysis: a response to Joan Hoff', *Women's History Review*, 5:1 (1996), pp. 19–23.

36. Joan Hoff, 'A reply to my critics', ibid., pp. 25–31.

37. Mary Maynard, 'Beyond the "Big Three": the development of feminist theory in the 1990s', *Women's History Review*, 4:3 (1995), pp. 259–81.

38. Kathleen Canning, 'Feminist history after the linguistic turn: historicizing discourse and experience', *Signs*, 19:2 (Winter, 1994), pp. 368–404.

39. Maynard (1995), p. 272.

40. Ronit Lentin, ed., *Gender and Catastrophe* (London, 1997), p. 5.

41. Ibid.

42. Joan Ringelheim, 'Genocide and gender: a split memory', in ibid., p. 32.

43. Sally Alexander, *Becoming a Woman and Other Essays* (London, 1994), p. xix.

44. Lyndal Roper, *Oedipus and the Devil: Witchcraft, Sexuality and Religion in Early Modern Europe* (London and New York, 1994), p. 3.

45. Lyndal Roper, *Holy Household: Women and Morals in Reformation Augsburg* (Oxford, 1989), p. 5.

46. Roper (1994), p. 26.

47. Ibid., p. 15.

48. Ibid., pp. 14–15.

49. Ibid., p. 15.

50. Ibid., p. 4.

51. Ibid., p. 17.

52. Ibid., p. 21.

53. Ibid., p. 11.

54. Ibid., p. 8.

55. Ibid., p. 18.

56. Joan Wallach Scott, ed., *Feminism and History* (Oxford, 1996).

57. Ibid., p. 11.

58. Ibid., p. 1.

59. Ibid., p. 13.

60. Ibid., p. 4.

61. Ibid., p. 5.

62. Ibid., p. 7.

63. Ibid., p. 8.

64. Kevin Passmore, *Women's History Review*, 7:2 (1998), pp. 261–5.

65. Lyn Hunt, 'Does history need defending?', *History Workshop Journal*, 46 (Autumn, 1998), pp. 241–51.

66. Michele Riot-Sarcey, 'Women's history in France: an ill-defined subject', *Gender & History*, 9:1 (April 1997), pp. 15–35.

67. Claire Midgeley, *Gender and Imperialism* (Manchester, 1997).

68. Ibid., p. 5.

69. Ibid.

70. Jane Haggis, 'White women and colonialism: towards a non-recuperative history', in ibid., pp. 63, 64.

71. Ibid., p. 64.

72. Ibid., p. 5.

73. Ibid., Joyce Appleby, Lynn Hunt and Margaret Jacob, *Telling the Truth About History* (New York and London, 1994).

74. Ibid., p. 235.

75. Ibid., pp. 258, 259.

76. Summerfield (1998), p. 10.

77. Ibid., p. 11.

78. Ibid., pp. 9–10.

79. Ibid., p. 12.

80. Ibid., pp. 15, 27.

81. Leonore Davidoff, *Worlds Between: Historical Perspectives on Gender and Class* (Cambridge, 1995).

82. Ibid., p. 1.

83. Ibid., p. 6.

84. Ibid., p. 7.

85. Ibid., pp. 11, 13.

86. Ibid., p. 14.

87. Gerda Lerner, *Why History Matters: Life and Thought* (Oxford and New York, 1997).

88. Ibid., p. 201.

89. Ibid.

90. Ibid., p. 203.

91. Ibid., pp. 204–5.

92. Ibid., p. 210.

93. Ibid., pp. xxxi–xxxii.

94. Ibid., p. xxxii.

95. Nathalie Zemon Davis, 'History's Two Bodies', *American Historical Review*, 93:1 (1988), p. 18.

96. Joan Wallach Scott, 'Rewriting History', in Margaret Higonnet, Jane Jenson, Sonya Michel and Margaret Weitz, eds., *Behind the Lines: Gender and the Two World Wars* (Yale, 1987), p. 22.

97. Zemon Davis (1988), p. 2.

98. Ibid., p. 2.

99. Scott (1987), p. 21.

100. Passmore (1998), p. 265.

BIBLIOGRAPHY

*Those book and article entries listed in **bold** are especially useful and influential.*

Books

Sally Alexander, *Becoming a Woman and Other Essays in Nineteenth and Twentieth Century Feminist History* (London, 1994)

Susan Amussen, *An Ordered Society: Gender and Class in Early Modern England* (London, 1993).

Bonnie Anderson and Judith Zinsser, *A History of Their Own* (London, 1988).

Joyce Appleby, Lyn Hunt and Margaret Jacob, *Telling the Truth About History* (New York, 1995).

Lois Banner, *Women in Modern America: A Brief History* (New York, 1984).

Mary Beard, *Woman as a Force in History* (New York, 1946).

Deirdre Beddoe, *Discovering Women's History* (London, 1983).

Judith Bennett, *Women in the Medieval Women's Countryside: Gender and Household in Brigstock Before the Plague* (Oxford, 1987).

Judith Bennett, *Ale, Beer and Brewsters in England: Women's Work in a Changing World* (Oxford, 1996).

Renate Bridhental and Claudia Koonz, eds., *Becoming Visible: Women in European History* (Boston, Mass., 1977).

Judith Butler, *Gender Trouble: Feminism and the Subversion of Identity* (London, 1990).

Judith Butler and Joan Scott, eds., *Feminists Theorize the Political* (London, 1992).

Berenice Carroll, ed., *Liberating Women's History* (Urbana and Chicago, Illinois, and London, 1976).

Alice Clark, *The Working Life of Women in the Seventeenth Century* (London, 1919).

Linda Colley, *Britons: Forging the Nation 1707–1837* (London, 1992).

Nancy Cott, *The Bonds of Womanhood* (New Haven, Conn., 1977).

Nancy Cott, *The Grounding of Modern Feminism* (New Haven, Conn., 1987).

Leonore Davidoff and Catherine Hall, *Family Fortunes: Men and Women of the English Middle Class 1780–1850* (London, 1987).

Leonore Davidoff, *Worlds Between: Historical Perspectives on Gender and Class* (Cambridge, 1995)

Teresa de Lauretis, ed., *Feminist Studies/Critical Studies* (Indiana, 1986).

Georges Duby and Michelle Perrot, eds., *A History of Women in the West* (Cambridge, Mass., 1992–4).

Linda Gordon, *Women's Body, Women's Right* (New York, 1976).

Linda Gordon, *Heroes of Their Own Lives: The Politics and History of Family Violence* (New York, 1988).

Catherine Hall, *White, Male and Middle-Class: Explorations in Feminism and History* (Cambridge, 1992).

Mary Hartman and Lois Banner, eds., *Clio's Consciousness Raised: New Perspectives on the History of Women* (New York, 1974).

Margaret Randolph Higonnet, Jane Jenson, Sonya Michel and Margaret Collins Weitz, eds., *Behind the Lines: Gender and Two World Wars* (New Haven, Conn., 1987).

Sandra Stanley Holton, *Feminist and Democracy* (Cambridge, 1986).

Olwen Hufton, *The Prospect Before Her: A History of Women in Western Europe, 1500–1800* (London, 1995).

Angela V. John and Claire Eustance, eds., *The Men's Share? Masculinities, Male Support and Women's Suffrage in Britain, 1890–1920* (London and New York, 1997).

Susan Kingsley Kent, *Sex and Suffrage in Britain, 1860–1914* (Princeton, New Jersey, 1987).

Susan Kingsley Kent, *Making Peace: the Reconstruction of Gender in Interwar Britain* (New Jersey, 1993).

Jay Kleinberg, ed., *Retrieving Women's History: Changing Perceptions of the Role of Women in Politics and Society* (Oxford and New York, 1988).

Joan Landes, *Women in the Public Sphere in the Age of Revolution* (Ithaca, NY, 1988).

Ronit Lentin, ed., *Gender and Catastrophe* (London, 1997).

Gerda Lerner, *The Majority Finds Its Past* (Oxford, 1979).

Gerda Lerner, *The Creation of Patriarchy* (Oxford, 1986).

Gerda Lerner, *The Creation of Feminist Consciousness* (Oxford, 1993).

Gerda Lerner, *Why History Matters: Life and Thought* (Oxford and New York, 1997).

Claire Midgeley, *Gender and Imperialism* (Manchester, 1997).

Rosamund Miles, *The Women's History of the World* (London, 1988).

Judith Newton, Mary Ryan and Judith Walkowitz, eds., *Sex and Class in Women's History* (London, 1983).

Karen Offen, Ruth Roach Pearson and Jane Rendall, *Writing Women's History: International Perspectives* (Basingstoke, 1991).

Alex Owen, *The Darkened Room: Women, Power and Spiritualism in Late Victorian England* (London, 1989).

Michelle Perrot, ed., *Writing Women's History* (Oxford, 1984).

Ivy Pinchbeck, *Women Workers and the Industrial Revolution* (London, 1930).

Mary Poovey, *Uneven Developments* (London, 1989).

June Purvis, ed., *Women's History: Britain 1850–1945: an introduction* (London, 1995).

Denise Riley, *Am I That Name?: Feminism and the Category of 'Women' in History* (London, 1988).

Lyndal Roper, *Holy Household: Women and Morals in Reformation Augsburg* (Oxford, 1989).

Lyndal Roper, *Oedipus and the Devil: Witchcraft, Sexuality and Religion in Early Modern Europe* (London and New York, 1994).

Michelle Zimbalist Rosaldo and Louise Lamphere, eds., *Women, Culture and Society* (Stanford, 1974).

Sheila Rowbotham, *Hidden from History* (London, 1973).

Sheila Rowbotham, *Woman's Consciousness, Man's World* (London, 1973).

Sheila Rowbotham, *Dreams and Dilemmas* (London, 1983).

Mary Ryan, *The Empire of the Mother: American Writing about Domesticity, 1830–1860* (New York, 1982).

Raphael Samuel, ed., *People's History and Socialist History* (London, 1989).

Joan Wallach Scott, *Gender and the Politics of History* (New York, 1988).

Carroll Smith-Rosenberg, *Disorderly Conduct: Visions of Gender in Victorian America* (Oxford, 1985).

Joan Wallach Scott, *Feminism & History* (Oxford, 1998).

Dale Spender, *Men's Studies Modified* (Oxford, 1981).

Liz Stanley, *The Auto/Biographical I: The Theory and Practice of Feminist Auto/Biography* (Manchester, 1992).

Penny Summerfield, *Reconstructing Women's Wartime Lives* (Manchester and New York, 1998).

John Tosh, *A Man's Place: Masculinity and the Middle-Class Home in Victorian England* (New Haven, Conn., 1999).

John Tosh and Michael Roper, eds., *Manful Assertions: Masculinities in Britian Since 1800* (London, 1991).

Amanda Vickery, *The Gentleman's Daughter: Women's Lives in Georgian England* (New Haven, Conn., 1998).

Judith Walkowitz, *Prostitution and Victorian Society* (Cambridge, 1978).

Vron Ware, *Beyond the Pale* (London, 1992).

Merry Wiesner, *Gender, Church and State in Early Modern Germany* (London and New York, 1988).

Articles

Sally Alexander, 'Women, class and sexual difference: some reflections on the writing of feminist history', *History Workshop Journal*, 17 (Spring 1984), pp. 125–49.

Valerie Amos and Pratibha Parmar, 'Challenging imperial feminisms', *Feminist Review*, 17 (Autumn 1984), pp. 3–19.

Lois Banner, 'A reply to 'Culture et pouvoir', *Journal of Women's History*, 1:1 (1989), pp. 101–7.

Elsa Barkley Brown, 'Polyrhythms and improvisation: lessons for women's history', *History Workshop Journal*, 31 (Spring 1991), pp. 85–91.

Judith Bennett, 'History that stands still: women's work in the European past', *Feminist Studies*, 14:2 (1988), pp. 269–83.

Judith Bennett, 'Feminism and history', *Gender & History*, 1:3 (1989), pp. 251–72.

Judith Bennett, 'Women's history: a study in continuity and change', *Women's History Review*, 2:2 (1993), pp. 173–85.

Gisela Bock, 'Women's history and gender history: aspects of an international debate', *Gender & History*, 1:1 (Spring 1989), pp. 7–30.

Mineke Bosch, 'The future of women's history: a Dutch perspective', *Gender & History*, 3:2 (Summer 1991), pp. 139–46.

Antoinette Burton, 'The white woman's burden: British feminists and the Indian woman, 1865–1915', *Women's Studies International Forum*, 13:4 (Winter 1990), pp. 293–308.

Antoinette Burton, 'The feminist quest for identity: British imperial suffragists, 1900–1915', *Journal of Women's History*, 3:2 (Summer 1991), pp. 46–81.

Antoinette Burton, 'History is now: feminist theory and the production of historical feminisms', *Women's History Review*, 1:1 (1992), pp. 25–38.

Kathleen Canning, 'Dialogue: the turn to gender and the challenge of poststructuralism', *Journal of Women's History*, 5:1 (Spring 1993), pp. 104–13.

Kathleen Canning, 'Feminist history after the linguistic turn: historicizing discourse and experience', *Signs*, 19:2 (1994), pp. 368–404.

Sue Clegg, 'The feminist challenge to socialist history', *Women's History Review*, 6:2 (1997), pp. 201–13.

Cecile Dauphin, Arlette Farge *et al.*, 'Women's culture and women's power: issues in French women's history', *Journal of Women's History*, 1:1 (Spring 1989), pp. 63–88.

Anna Davin, 'Imperialism and motherhood', *History Workshop Journal*, 5 (1978), pp. 9–65.

Nathalie Zemon Davis, ' "Women's history" in transition: the European case', *Feminist Studies*, 3:3/4 (Spring/Summer 1976), pp. 83–103.

Nathalie Zemon Davis, 'History's two bodies', *American Historical Review*, 93:1 (1988), pp. 1–31.

Ellen Dubois, 'Politics and culture in women's history', *Feminist Studies*, 6:1 (Spring 1980).

Richard Evans, 'Women's history: the limits of reclamation', *Social History*, v:2 (May 1980), pp. 273–81.

Catherine Hall, 'Politics, poststructuralism and feminist history', *Gender & History*, 3:2 (Summer 1991), pp. 204–10.

Brian Harrison and James McMillan, 'Some feminist betrayals of women's history', *Historical Journal*, 25:2 (1982), pp. 501–12.

Evelyn Brooks Higginbotham, 'African–American women's history: the junction of race and class', *Signs*, 17:2 (Winter 1992), pp. 251–74.

Bridget Hill, 'Women's history: a study in continuity, change or standing still?', *Women's History Review*, 2:1 (1993), pp. 5–22.

Darlene Clark Hine, 'Black women's history, white women's history: the junction of race and class', *Journal of Women's History*, 4:2 (Autumn, 1992), pp. 125–33.

Joan Hoff, 'Gender as a postmodern category of paralysis', *Women's History Review*, 3:2 (1994), pp. 149–68.

Joan Hoff, 'A reply to my critics', *Women's History Review*, 5:1 (1996), pp. 25–31.

Olwen Hufton, 'What is women's history?', *History Today* (June 1985), pp. 38–40.

Kali A.K. Israel, 'Writing inside the kaleidoscope: re-representing Victorian women public figures', *Gender & History*, 2:1 (Spring 1990), pp. 40–8.

Joan Kelly, 'The social relations of the sexes: methodological implications of women's history', *Signs*, 1:4 (Summer 1976), pp. 809–23.

Joan Kelly, 'The doubled vision of feminist theory', *Feminist Studies*, 5:1 (Spring 1979), pp. 216–27.

Susan Kingsley Kent, 'Mistrals and distribulations: a reply to Joan Hoff', *Women's History Review*, 5:1 (1996), pp. 9–18.

Gerda Lerner, 'The lady and the mill girl: changes in the status of women in the age of Jackson', *Midcontinent American Studies Journal*, 10 (Spring, 1969).

Gerda Lerner, 'New approaches to the study of women in American history', *Journal of Social History*, 3:1 (1969), pp. 53–62.

Gerda Lerner, 'The majority finds its past', *Current History*, 70:416 (May, 1976), pp. 194–6.

Gerda Lerner, 'Placing women in history: definitions and challenges', *Feminist Studies*, 5:1/2 (Spring/Summer 1978), pp. 5–14.

Tessa Liu, 'Teaching differences among women from a historical perspective', *Women's Studies International Forum*, 14:4 (Winter 1991), pp. 265–76.

Mary Maynard, 'Beyond the "Big Three": the development of feminist theory in the 1990s', *Women's History Review*, 4:3 (1995), pp. 259–81.

Louise Newman, 'Dialogue: critical theory and the history of women: what's at stake in deconstructing women's history', *Journal of Women's History*, 2:3 (Winter 1991), pp. 58–68.

Judith Newton, 'Dialogue: critical theory and the history of women: what's at stake in deconstructing women's history', *Journal of Women's History*, 2:3 (Winter 1991), p. 102.

Karen Offen, 'A historically based definition of feminism', *Signs*, 14 (Autumn 1988), pp. 149–57.

Ruth Perry, 'Women and Daughters', *History Workshop Journal*, 47 (Spring 1999), pp. 292–6.

Mary Poovey, 'Feminism and deconstruction', *Feminist Studies*, 14:1 (Spring 1988), pp. 52–65.

Caroline Ramazanoglu, 'Unravelling postmodern paralysis: a response to Joan Hoff', *Women's History Review*, 5:1 (1996), pp. 19–23.

Rayna Rapp, Ellen Ross and Renate Bridenthal, 'Examining Family History', *Feminist Studies*, 5:1 (Spring 1979), pp. 174–96.

Michelle Zimbalist Rosaldo, 'The use and abuse of anthropology', *Signs*, 5 (Spring 1980), pp. 400–14.

Ute Schmidt, 'Problems of theory and method in feminist history', in Joanna de Groot and Mary Maynard, eds., *Women's Studies in the 1990s: Doing Things Differently* (Basingstoke, 1993).

Joan Scott and Louise Tilly, 'Women's work and the family in nineteenth-century Europe', *Comparative Studies in Society and History*, 17 (January 1975).

Joan Scott, 'Women in history: the modern period', *Past and Present*, 101 (1983), pp. 141–57.

Joan Scott, 'Gender: a useful category of historical analysis', *American Historical Review*, 91:5 (1986), pp. 1053–75.

Barbara Sicherman, 'American history', *Signs*, 1:1 (Winter, 1975), pp. 461–85.

Bonnie Smith, 'Seeing Mary Beard', *Feminist Studies*, 10:3 (Autumn, 1984), pp. 399–418.

Bonnie Smith, 'The contribution of women to modern historiography in Great Britain, France and the United States, 1750–1940', *American Historical Review*, p. 89 (1986).

Carroll Smith-Rosenberg, 'The new woman and the new history', *Feminist Studies*, 3:2 (Autumn 1975a), pp. 185–98.

Carroll Smith-Rosenberg, 'The female world of love and ritual', *Signs*, 1:3 (Autumn 1975b), pp. 1–29.

Carroll Smith-Rosenberg, 'Politics and culture in women's history', *Feminist Studies*, 6:1 (Spring 1980).

Liz Stanley, ed., 'British Feminist Histories', *Women's Studies International Forum*, 13 (1990).

John Tosh, 'What should historians do with masculinity?', *History Workshop Journal*, 38 (1994), pp. 179–202.

Amanda Vickery, 'Golden Age to Separate Spheres? A review of the categories and chronology of English women's history', *Historical Journal*, 36:2 (1993), pp. 283–414.

Judith Walkowitz, 'Introduction to "Politics and Culture in Women's History"', *Feminist Studies*, 6:1 (Spring 1980).

Judith Walkowitz, 'Patrolling the borders of feminist historiography and the new historicism', *Radical History Review*, 43 (1989), pp. 23–43.

INDEX

Abbott, Edith
Women in Industry (1918) 7
Abensour, Leon
*La Femme et le féminisme en France avant la
Revolution* (1923) 41
Alexander, Sally 28 (ment.), 29, 52, 64,
77, 136
*Becoming a Woman and and Other Essays on
19th and 20th Century Feminist History*
(1994) 55–6, 131
'Women, class and sexual differences
in the 1830s and 1840s: Some
reflections on the writing of feminist
history' (1984) 55–6
'Women's work in nineteenth-century
London: A study of the years
1820–50' (1976) 27, 43
Alexander, Sally & Taylor, Barbara
'In defence of patriarchy' (1979) 43
Amos, Valerie 112
Amussen, Susan 116
*An Ordered Society: Gender and Class in Early
Modern England* (1988) 94
Anderson, Bonnie & Zinsser, Judith
A History of Their Own (1998) 94–5
anthropology
impetus for women's studies 30. *See also*
women's historiography, models,
anthropological/ethnohistorical
Appleby, Joyce, *et al.*
Telling the Truth About History (1994) 135

Bakhtin, M. 75
Banner, Lois
Women in Modern America: A Brief History
(1974) 29
'A reply to "Culture et pouvoir"
from the perspective of
United States women's history'
(1989) 91–2
Barkley Brown, Elsa. *See* Brown, Elsa
Barkley

Baxandall, Rosalyn (1939–)
'Women in American trade unions'
(1976) 27
Beard, Mary (1876–1958) 1 (ment.), 97
on female historical perspective 8
responses to her writings 8
America Through Women's Eyes (1933) 8
On Understanding Women (1931) 8
Women as a Force in History (1946) 7–8
Bennett, Judith 23, 95–6, 97
challenged 115
response to challenge 115–16
commitment to feminism 16
Ale and Beer (1996) 116
Feminism and History (1989) 93
*Women in the Medieval Countryside: Gender
and Household in Brigstock before the
Plague* (1987) 93–4
Berkshire Women's History
Conferences 23, 41, 118
binary oppositions
defined 64
problems with 109
Bock, Gisela 105, 109
on concept of gender 16
'Women's history and gender history:
aspects of an international debate'
(1989) 92, 123
'Challenging dichotomies:
developments in women's
history' (1991) 105–6
Bosch, Mineke 114, 117
'The future of women's history'
(1991) 106
Brown, Elsa Barkley 112, 114
Buhle, Mary-Jo (1943–) 24
on Dubois 49
Butler, Judith 135
deconstruction, proponent of 108–9
on colonialism and oppression 115
*Gender Trouble: Feminism and the Subversion
of Identity* (1990) 108–9

historians of women 82–3, 111
  American 3–4, 11–13, 14
    challenging male paradigms 50
    gender 57
  British 3–7
    class issue 50, 57
    marginalised 16, 51, 111
    and Marxism 26–7
  cooperative not competitive 45,
    138
  French 4, 14–15, 91, 133–4
    embattled 89
    cultural approach 90
    historiographical framework 16
  male 69
  see also under name
historian's task 9
historical analysis
  multi-disciplinary approach 17
  see also historical concepts; women's
    historiography
historical concepts
  agency 18, 26
  Freudian 26
  gender 105, 106, 139
    acceptance of 36, 53–4, 93
    agreement on use 98
    attraction of 139
    and class 50
    problems of 16, 95–6, 126–7
    defined 14, 63, 64, 88
    importance of 42, 70, 76, 77, 78
    race 102
    see also gender groups, historical
      significance
  experience 18
  the family 55
  the individual 18
  language 74
  material forces
    importance of 17
  matriarchy
    idealised 4
  patriarchy
    and biological determinism 14
    challenged 43, 63, 115
    defined 29
    defended 43, 96
    validity of concept 16, 115–16
    and women's history 93
  periodisation 42, 46
  power 22, 26, 64
  separate spheres, public/private 32, 46,
    63, 90–1, 98

subordination/oppression, instability of
    terms 31
  women, instability of term 22, 25
  see also patriarchy, as a system of social
    control
historical sources
  archival/original documents 4, 105
    Foucault on 128
  demographic 5, 41
  didactic 46
  expansion of 65
  experiences 107–8
  interpretation of 53, 56
  literary 84, 105
  materials of culture 105
  new types 56
  printed 64–5, 117
  personal/private materials 4, 46
    validity defended 3
  women's voices 32
  working-class women, lack of for 35
historiography
  Annales/mentalité 13, 69
  family history 53
  gender and 87, 88, 92–3, 94
  impact of women's history 12, 13, 56,
    86–8
  labour history, omission of women 53
  Lacan's model 64
  linguistic turn 129–30
    defined 17
  mid-twentieth century 8–9
  origins of modern 2. *See also* von Ranke,
    historiographical legacy
  women's, absence of 66
  see also historical concepts; women's
    historiography
history
  1960s Oxford curriculum 9–10
history of women. *See* women's
    historiography
History Workshop Journal 52–3
Hoff, Joan 17, 135
  'Gender as a postmodern category of
    paralysis' (1994) 126–7
    reply to 127
Holton, Sandra Stanley
  Feminist Democracy (1986) 73–4
Horney, Karen 31
Hufton, Olwen 17
  *The Prospect Before Her: A History of Women
    in Western Europe, 1500–1800*
    (1995) 125–6
  'What is women's history?' (1985) 69

Utopian socialism 63

Vicinus, Martha 77
  Suffer and be Still: Women in the Victorian Age
    (1972) 30
Vickery, Amanda
  The Gentleman's Daughter: Women's Live in
    Georgian England (1998) 116–17
  'Golden Age to Separate Spheres? A
    review of the categories and
    chronology of English women's
    history' (1993) 116–17

Walkowitz, Judith 51, 57, 62, 63, 77, 88
  on the enterprise of women's history
    85–6
  City of Dreadful Delight: Narratives of Sexual
    Danger in late-Victorian London (1992)
    85
Ware, Vron
  Beyond the Pale (1992) 113
Wells, Ida B. 113
Welter, Barbara (1967–)
  The Cult of True Womanhood, 1820–1860
    (1966) 11
White, Haydn 75, 134
Wiesner, Merry 136
  Gender, Church and State in Early Modern
    Germany (1998) 122
Willard, Frances Elizabeth Caroline (1839–
    1898) and Livermore, Mary Ashton
    (1820–1905)
  American Women (1897) 3
women
  Black American 57
  historical contribution of 23
  history of, absence from 10, 29
    challenged 10–12
  instability of term 22, 25, 87, 104
  self-awareness awakened 7
  see also; historians of women; publishing,
    women's; women's historiography
women's historiography 1, 9, 11–13, 21, 28
  acceptance of 53, 65, 122
    in Britain 66, 111
  Black women, absence of 104, 105
  Communist Party's historians' group 28
  compensatory history 33
  complexities of 22–3, 42, 44, 45, 102
  contribution history 34, 45
    'women worthies' 41
  definition 70
  discipline, place in broader 95
    impact of 13, 18, 40–1, 62, 122
  encouragement of/support for 6, 29

feminist perspective 15, 22, 47–8, 92
  challenged 70–2
  definition of 72–3
  destabilising force 109
  ethnocentrism/racism of 111, 113–15
  and gender 83, 117
  radical 44
  suspicion of 28, 33, 54
  tensions, source of 70
  in France 14–15, 133–4
  gender history, displaced by 110
  goals 41
  growth of 53, 56
  Hartman, Mary on 23
  impetus for 3, 12, 24 33, 97, 138, 139
  importance of 117–18
  Lerner, Gerda on 22–3
  men, extended to 70
  methodologies 2–5, 65
    borrowed from other disciplines 12
    problems with existing 41, 53
  models 22, 26, 34
    anthropological/ethnohistorical 30, 35
      misused 43–4
    Derridean (deconstruction) 74, 78, 87
    feminist/socialist 29, 24–5, 47–50
    literary 83, 85–6
    Foucauldian 50–1, 87, 88, 105
    gender-based 45, 57, 61
    Marxist 27, 28, 34, 43, 44, 63
    multiple, room for 102–4, 106–7,
      122–3, 132–3, 138
    poststructuralist 85–6, 76
      unsuitability of 102
    psychoanalytical/psychological 31, 35
      Lacanian 64
    woman-centred 24–5, 53, 54
  patriarchy. *see* historical concepts,
    patriarchy
  periodisation 34
  race, impact on 112–14
  radical potential 63
  responses to 8, 11, 29
  rigour of 54, 135
  significance of 21
  subjectivity 55
  tradition, lack of 42, 61
  validity of 32, 64, 70
  see also historical concepts; historians of
    women; historiography

Zemon Davis, Natalie. *See* Davis, Natalie
  Zemon
Zinsser, Judith. *See* Anderson, Bonnie &
  Zinsser, Judith